A Woma

Empowering Female
to Authentically Le
in a Man's

Michelle R. Donovan & Patty Kreamer

First Edition

Publish Connect * Houston * PA

A Woman's Way

Empowering female financial advisors
to authentically lead and flourish in a man's world

Michelle R. Donovan & Patty Kreamer

Published by:
Publish Connect
Houston, PA

ISBN: 978-0-9720001-9-2 (Paperback)

Library of Congress Cataloging-in-Publication Data

Donovan, Michelle R. & Kreamer, Patty
A Woman's Way
Empowering Female Financial Advisors
to Authentically Lead and Flourish in a Man's World
Library of Congress Control Number: 2018947921

We dedicate this book to the women of
wealth management around the world.

TABLE OF CONTENTS

A few notes:

In doing research for this book, we discovered the financial planning and advisor world is referred to as both an industry and a profession.

In the research literature, women are referred to as women financial advisors, women advisors, female advisors and female financial advisors.

You will see a variety of these terms scattered throughout this book.

ACKNOWLEDGEMENTS

Thank you to all the women advisors who took time out of their day to share their stories with us.

Thank you to those leading the way to create more inclusive and welcoming environments for women advisors.

Thank you to our clients who inspire and motivate us every day.

Thank you to our family and friends for their belief in our vision.

Thank you to our editor Chris Abbott for her expertise, excellent eye and awesome sister.

Thank you to Mary Malinconico for saving the day with our cover. We now know better.

And thank you to Stephen Eckert for his ongoing wisdom, support and insight that kept this important project moving forward.

WHY THIS BOOK WAS WRITTEN

You are a woman in a man's industry. Everything you've been taught to start your career as a female financial advisor has come to you mainly from the men in your industry. Men have been the dominating force in the financial world for a long, long time. They have the experience and the success to prove they know what they're doing.

Given the male-dominated history of the financial planning industry, then, it is not surprising that so many female financial advisors feel disconnected with how they go about growing and managing their practice. Neither is it surprising to hear women advisors respond to male ways of working as prickly as wearing a burlap dress. A man's way of work, however good for him, is not your way of work. A man's way of acquiring business is not your way of acquiring business. A man's client approach is not your client approach. A man's way of managing his practice is not necessarily the way you want to manage your practice.

Sure, you can learn to adapt everything about yourself in order to fit into this man's world. You can learn to speak to clients like men do. You can learn to bring in referrals like men do. You can learn to grow your practice like men do. You can adapt yourself to learn the systems and processes that men use. But in what ways might these adaptations compromise your authenticity?

We have a better option. You can learn to trust WHO and WHAT you are to grow and manage a financial practice far beyond what you could ever imagine today. We've seen it happen! We've helped it happen with our clients. *A Woman's Way* of working is simply different than a man's way. It's not inferior, just different. *A Woman's Way* of asking for referrals is comfortable for her. *A Woman's Way* of developing relationships is different than a man's way and should be leveraged strategically. The natural way you create a process is the way that's best for you.

This book has been written to serve you and be your guide as you navigate the male-dominated worlds of financial planning and wealth management. We know you've experienced a situation similar to that depicted on the cover of this book - standing out in a sea of sameness. Being the only women in a room of dark suits and ties is not uncommon. That's why **Section One** of this book helps you realize that you're definitely not alone. After interviewing dozens of female financial advisors from around the country, we identified common themes, issues, struggles, and strengths. These conversations affirmed for us that women financial advisors should first be validated for what they experience in a man's world. Our research also allows us to address where women advisors currently find support and where they still need backing. We found it intriguing to hear women advisors share why they feel more women are not in this profession and why they feel they should be. In fact, if your firm is trying to attract more women, it might be valuable to share this section with the leadership as direct insight from the field.

Section Two highlights your natural strengths as a woman and shows how these strengths can and will be instrumental in building your practice your way, *A Woman's Way*. We take a close look at how perfectly aligned you are to be a wildly successful financial advisor just by being you. Emphasizing the inherent talents of women professionals builds an even stronger case for increasing the number of women in the wealth management profession.

Section Three looks inward and begins to focus directly on you. This is where the work begins, complete with action steps, to instill a level of accountability. This section addresses the internal barriers and saboteurs faced by women advisors as revealed by women advisors themselves. We dig deep into the darkest corners of what really gets in the way of your productivity and offer many solutions to move you forward. As the starting point of breaking through the internal barriers that block you from fulfilling your professional goals, it's important to be 100% honest when reading this section. To address the nagging issue of work/life balance, we give you valuable insights and strategies on how even you can be more productive, ultimately freeing up time for what matters most in your life.

In **Section Four**, we look closely at the lifeblood of your business – relationships and referrals. This section walks you through specific referral approaches that other female advisors like you have found to be effective, productive, and most importantly, feel right, too. We'll show you how to capitalize on your authentic self to grow your practice your way, *A Woman's Way*. And we certainly can't let you get away without working through action steps here as well to create new tools to improve your referability.

In **Section Five** you'll hear the voices of the women we interviewed speaking to you as if you were sitting together over coffee or lunch. Their valuable insights spread over various topics--all meaningful, regardless of whether you're newer to the profession or a 20-year veteran. You will feel the common sisterhood of *A Woman's Way* and nod your head in affirmation of the incredible spirit inherent in woman's power.

Our first goal for you with this book is that you build a practice you're proud of in a manner that supports who you are naturally as a woman.

Our second goal for you is that you build a practice that supports your life ambitions, regardless of how you define them.

Our third goal for you is that you become inspired to support the other women advisors around you. Just as it takes a "village to raise a child," it takes a community of giving, successful women advisors to stand behind the next generation of female advisors, ultimately impacting the balance of men and women in your profession.

We believe strongly that if women advisors are going to be successful in a male-dominated profession, they must support each other and their successes. Women need to lead the way by helping other women appreciate and consider the financial profession as a viable way to make life-changing impacts on people around the world. Recent history reminds us that WOMEN'S POWER is truly impressive and can be responsible for real social and economic change.

You don't have to look too far back in history to find how women banding together can change the fabric of a culture. In late 2017, the *#MeToo* movement began and went viral in an effort to demonstrate the widespread prevalence of sexual misconduct, assault and harassment against women, especially in the workplace. This movement continues to heighten everyone's awareness of the many injustices that are now front and center in the media. In response to this wake-up call, the Time's Up movement was announced on January 1, 2018 to support those who have less access to media platforms and the funds necessary to speak up about gender harassment.

As these social movements demonstrate, however, it will take your willingness to band together on behalf of your sisterhood to propel women forward in this profession.

So, sit back and dig in your heels (if you wear them). This book could (and should) change the way you're doing business right now. It might stretch you a bit and challenge you to increase your confidence in knowing (not just suspecting, but really knowing in your heart) that YOUR way – *A Woman's Way* – is a profitable way to grow and productively manage a financial planning business. If you're ready, let's embrace and cultivate *A Woman's Way*.

SECTION 1

Face the Wind

External barriers faced by women advisors

"The cards are stacked against you girl, get back in bed."
- Mary Chapin Carpenter

Some days you might just want to get back in bed. It's tough out there, and this is no surprise to you because you're living it every day. You attend conferences surrounded by a sea of black suits and often times consider yourself lucky if you get to hear two or three women speak from the platform. In your office or firm, you might even be the only woman advisor on the team or one of a few in your entire region. In meetings, sometimes you can count the number of women advisors on one hand. One.

The 2014 CFP® Board study titled, "Making More Room for Women in the Financial Planning Profession," discussed various ways that the odds are stacked against you. In addition, our interviews with women advisors both confirmed these barriers and added a few to the list. This section focuses on current dominating external barriers facing female financial advisors that we believe could and should be addressed systemically by the leading influencers throughout the profession:

- Gender bias and discrimination
- Scarcity of female role models
- Work and life balance expectations
- Sexual harassment

Let's take a few minutes to reflect on these obstacles and recognize the impact each is having on women advisors.

Gender bias and discrimination

The CFP® Board study showed that in the financial planning profession, men typically are sought out more, hired more, and paid more. Granted, currently there are certainly more men to choose from when looking to fill a position or expand a firm. However, this discrepancy merely begs the question; how do we attract more women to the profession? Regarding gender bias, the statistics are stunning. It's been shown that when performing the same tasks, women advisors earn on average $32,000/year less than male advisors, and they are significantly less likely to own their own practice (only 39% of women own their own or part of a practice compared to 63% of men). One of the women we interviewed knew these statistics well and commented, "When women make an average of 20-30% or 30K less than men, it makes you feel less than and it is a big reason that keeps women out."

In a December 2016 article posted on *Forbes.com*, the salary information site PayScale identified the overall gender pay gap was 24 percent. Leading the pack by industry were finance and insurance with a gap of 29.1%. In another article from *Bustle.com*, Erin McKelle Fischer quoted the 2015 U.S. Census data, which also uncovered the guiltiest industry for gender pay gaps - the financial service industry. In 2015, female securities and commodities brokers earned an average of 54 percent of their male counterparts, while female financial specialists on Wall Street earned an average of 60 percent of their male counterparts. And female financial advisors earned 62 cents on a man's dollar.

Many women we spoke to seemed to share a common feeling that financially, this is not a business for the faint of heart. We heard comments like this one repeated several times: "It's hard financially to build a business. It seems to be best if you have another income behind you." The male/female compensation disparity impacts women throughout their careers. Not only do women bring home less money than men, but the ripple effect impacts their ability to save for retirement.

Throughout the industry's history, some women advisors have made it well known that gender bias won't be tolerated when it comes to compensation dispensation and that this sisterhood can make a significant impact. In 2007, seven women advisor plaintiffs filed a class action lawsuit against a top wirehouse claiming gender discrimination. The suit was filed on behalf of themselves and nearly 4,800 other former and current employees of this institution. It was alleged that their employer had established policies that caused their compensation to fall below their male counterparts. The women plaintiffs claimed that account distribution policies as well as how teams were formed both favored men and positioned them to receive higher pay. The wirehouse agreed to pay 39 million dollars to resolve the lawsuit.

In a February 25, 2011 article by Jerry Gleeson on *WealthManagement.com*, the author pointed out that throughout the years millions and millions of dollars have been spent to settle cases focused on gender bias and/or discrimination. Specifically, between 1996 and 2011, nearly 400 million dollars were paid out in lawsuits from large wirehouses fighting cases of discrimination. One would think that an industry full of holes from the buckshot of gender inequality lawsuits combined with the desperate need for more women in the ranks would rally together for systemic change. Sadly, an unbalanced compensation structure that appears to reflect gender bias simply promotes women to turn in another direction.

In addition to the compensation disparity problems, many women struggle with the commission-based sales model still seen in many wirehouses and financial firms. One advisor told us, "Women can't afford to give up their good salary to become an advisor; it's not worth it to them." Yet another stated, "Women advisors who go to wirehouses set themselves up for failure. They go to a wirehouse expecting to get support and then they don't get it." More often than not, there are promises of support, training, and a salary for a given period of time. However, many women soon discover that the reality of the situation turns out to be a very painful environment of loneliness, isolation, stress, and uncomfortable sales strategies that do not fit with their relationship-based needs. We have heard similar sentiments reflected from those we spoke to for this book.

- "Women need a paycheck! The model is not set up for women. Dialing for dollars provides no connection to the prospect."

- "It's about sales from day one. Women won't bet on themselves like men will. Women do not like to be perceived as 'salesy.'"

- "Commission sales are tough! Some can't make ends meet."

- "Women don't have the time or luxury that it takes to build up a book of business for significant revenue."

- "It takes years to build the experience and the revenue. Women are not going to make much money fast and this is viewed as a detriment."

- "It's a big risk. Women are risk-averse. They need to take care of their family. To work hard, the family suffers. If you get no new clients, you've just worked really hard with nothing to show for your efforts."

- "It's particularly hard for a young woman to get in the business with 100% commission and student loans weighing on her shoulders."

Gender bias is one thing when it comes to compensation structures. Being taken seriously as a woman in a man's world is yet another way women are constantly battling for credibility. This issue still exists in 2018 and it is felt completely across the male board from upper management, colleagues, centers of influence (COIs), and even clients. It's hard to imagine that in 2018 women advisors are still being called "honey" and "sweetie" while being asked to retrieve coffee for everyone (all the men) as if they are assistants rather than equals. And it's discouraging to hear that clients still walk away from the table because the advisor is a woman.

Imagine the level of frustration a woman advisor must deal with when she is treated as though she has no value.

Imagine the level of exhaustion a woman advisor must experience from needing to constantly prove herself to others and then again to herself.

Imagine the level of discomfort a woman advisor must tolerate being invisible in a room flooded with dark suits where everyone is shaking hands except with her.

One of our interviewees said it best, "Women who succeed are made of steel."

Please don't think that every male in this profession contributes to this type of treatment towards women advisors. On the contrary. We personally know many, many men and firms who are incredibly supportive of women as advisors.

Many of the women we spoke to have experienced all the good that their firms have to offer. And equally so, many have experienced the bad along their path. It's these stories of struggle that we feel are particularly important to share in order to increase awareness that although some gender bias and discrimination have melted away, much of it is still lingering. In fact, many people told us they would not recommend this profession to other women they know because of these biases. Clearly, this reticence is counterproductive to what the financial profession is hoping to accomplish in the years ahead.

Listening to some real women advisor's thoughts, feelings, and experiences can be downright shocking. If you're reading this book as a woman advisor, what will you do if/when you experience this feeling or action? If you're reading this as the head of a firm, what can be done at your firm to ensure your women advisors never feel this way?

- "Being young and a woman, clients didn't see me as a subject matter expert. Now I know to stay out of the weeds."

- "Old men have old views of women. I keep my head down and don't rock the boat."

- "It feels like my opinion doesn't matter, especially if I'm put in front of a businessman over 50 who was raised in an environment where men pulled each other up and didn't respect what women said. I'm not given the same level of respect or credibility. I have to earn every bit of it."

- "Traditional male law firms don't see me as a resource or center of influence. The guys call me *Honey* or *Sweetie*."

- "Men are men with no professional boundaries. Many COIs look at lunch as a 'date.'"

- "I remember many times where I was not treated as an equal. The guys would shake everyone's hand in the room except mine. Instead, men treated me like I was the assistant, asking me to get coffee, etc."

- "It did not feel nice to be a woman at a conference. When I spoke at a conference, I felt I was up there and was not fully respected by my peers. It was not enjoyable at all and it felt as if I wasn't being taken seriously."

- "It's not as accepted to say what I think without being called a 'Bitch.'"

- "We fight harder for credibility. My revenue is always a surprise to the men."

- "Many men have an inappropriate view of women advisors especially when they are with another male advisor."

- "Going to conferences is like going to a meat market. As women, we learned the hard way to never go to an evening event/party alone. Sadly, new female advisors don't know this so it is up to us to warn them and watch their backs."

Scarcity of female role models

How easy is it for you to find a successful woman advisor in your company, firm, community or neighborhood whom you could visit and share best practices with to help you grow and manage your practice? Who could be your female mentor? Who helps you when you need to express your frustrations, fears, or share your successes?

According to the 2017 *InvestmentNews* "Adviser Compensation and Staffing Study," only about 16% of firm leaders are women. Typically, because women are scarce in the leadership role, female newcomers receive this kind of mentorship and support from men. Now please don't think we're men haters or male bashers. Quite the opposite is true! We believe wholeheartedly that you can and will learn a great deal from male advisors and mentors. That being said, the point to make is that in addition to men, women need other women to look up to, to use as sounding boards, to connect with and to learn from, and right now, there is a drought in this area.

In a *Financial Advisor* article from March 2018 titled, "Want More Women Advisors?" the 2016 Bureau of Labor Statistics lists the total number of female personal financial advisors at just 31.6% in the country. In 2017, the CFP® Board said the number of female CFP® professionals was stalled at 23%. The *Financial Advisor* article also interviewed several successful women advisors and asked what three things needed to happen to attract more women to the profession. Among its many opinions, the article made clear that if women don't see themselves represented in the profession they will not be interested in following that path. When women don't see other women being successful in their profession, they will convince themselves that success is not attainable.

The reality is that women connect differently to other women than they do with men, for there is a deeper level of mutual understanding. Without this layer of shared support in your career, you simply will feel the void and experience a sense of aloneness. What's more, not having other women as mentors and support turns out to actually be bad for your health!

In researching this topic, we discovered several studies and scholars who have proven that when women connect with other women for support, it's not only good for their business but it's good for their health as well. In an article posted on *HuffPost Women* in November 2012 called "A Compelling Argument About Why Women

Need Friendships" by Dr. Randy Kamen, several studies were highlighted. The first was a landmark study by Laura Klein and Shelley Taylor that revealed women need other women when they are experiencing stress. The authors stated: "When life becomes challenging, women seek out friendships with other women as a means of regulating stress levels. A common female stress response is to 'tend and befriend.' That is, when women become stressed, their inclination is to nurture those around them and reach out to others."

The second study noted in Kamen's article was referred to as the Nurses' Health Study from Harvard Medical School. This report showed "that the more friends women have, the less likely they are to develop physical impairments as they age and the more likely they are to lead a contented life." This study also showed that "not having friends or confidants is as detrimental to your health as being overweight or smoking cigarettes."

Total Health Magazine also featured an article called "Female Friendship Good for Your Health" by Gloria Gilbere, PhD that stated,

"Women connect with each other very differently — providing support systems that help each other deal with the stresses and difficult life experiences we all encounter. Physically, this quality 'girlfriend time' helps us to create more serotonin — a neurotransmitter that helps combat depression and can help create a general feeling of well-being."

For example, Michelle met with a woman advisor (we'll call her Karol) who had been a coaching client for several years. Through her coaching experience, she eventually left the banking environment as a financial advisor and (with an assistant) started a thriving advisor practice of her own. Despite everything that indicated she would flourish, Karol had been battling with the confidence necessary to believe she could actually make it on her own. She was stressed at the thought of being a business owner. One day when Michelle and Karol were having lunch, Karol looked at her new Fitbit heartrate monitor and said, "My heart rate while talking to you is lower now than it is when I wake up in the morning! How can that be?" You guessed it – serotonin. Girlfriend time creates this neurotransmitter in spades, and it simply does its thing to calm us down and relieve stress. Health professionals like Dr. Gilbere, along with our own experiences, lead us to conclude that if there are no other women advisors to reach out to and confide in, the stress levels for women advisors can become excessive and debilitating.

Other research sighted in this article directly showed the connection between female friendships and depression. In a nutshell, time with other females produces a beneficial hormone in the body that helps us stay calm, reduces anxiety, reduces stress, and increases the overall quality of our health. It would stand to reason then that a lack of female mentors and/or friends who can not only provide a willing ear but also relate to the pressures of your profession could severely impact both the success of women advisor practices and their overall health as well.

When we spoke to women currently in the profession, all agreed with the need to have a female support mechanism. Here are some of their thoughts on this issue when asked what advice they would share with younger women advisors:

- "I challenge other women advisors to step into leadership roles because other women advisors need to see you there. Be the change you seek and it will evoke change."

- "Find others who are like you."

- "Get involved in some industry groups."

- "You need people around you; don't do it alone."

- "Find someone with whom you can share successes and disappointments without worry."

- "Find an advocate if possible."

- "Find a mentor and find personal freedom."

- "Start to build your peer network NOW!"

In addition, the successful women advisors that we interviewed shared where they have found their support and who they have turned to for guidance. It should be noted that some women felt that they had great support from specific men in their firms who they say "get it." All seem to agree that having a stronger female advisor sisterhood of support would be a welcome asset to their success.

Here's a list of many of the current avenues for support that women advisors are leveraging today (in no certain order of priority):

- FPA – Financial Planning Association
- 100 Women in Finance – www.100women.org
- NAIFA – National Association of Insurance and Financial Advisors
- NAPFA - National Association of Personal Financial Advisors
- XY Planning Network
- FPA Retreat
- Women's Leadership Council
- PowerLink
- WIFS – Women in Insurance & Financial Services
- NAWBO – National Association of Women Business Owners
- WPO – Women Presidents' Organization
- Coaches
- Therapists
- Female partners in the firm
- Mentors (male & female)
- Spouse or partner
- Family
- Friends
- Co-workers

- Myself
- Trusted male advisors with good perspective
- Broker/dealer
- Study groups
- Colleagues from a past job or career

Erinn Ford, President of Cetera Advisors, states that broker/dealers need to "establish and invest in mentoring networks that align experienced women advisors with ones who are more junior. Ultimately, one of the most effective ways to inspire women in more junior roles to become successful advisors is by showing them real-life examples of women who have risen to the top." Ford believes it's important to "not leave it to luck for these mentoring interactions to happen."

Work/Life balance expectations

Smartphones at the dining room table, re-charging anxiously on your nightstand, and secured in the pocket, purse, holster or duffle bag of everyone you know – you, your partner, children, business associates and extended family – say it clearly. Our electronic connection to our world never stops. Work never stops. Today more than ever before, women and men are tethered to their work lives. Women advisors are no different. As the pressure to produce and service clients squeezes from all sides, so does the pressure to perform as a good parent, daughter, partner or spouse. Regardless of whether you are caring for children, parents, life partners, spouses, other family members, or even your beloved pets, the feeling of being squeezed in a vice encompasses us daily. How do we prioritize when everything and everyone is a priority?

The minute women began working outside of the home, the issue of work/life balance was born. There have been plenty of books written on the subject and many adjustments made throughout the ages to business work styles in an attempt to help women who struggle with balancing it all. Some of those work style adjustments have become very attractive to women, thereby swaying them towards careers in fields such as teaching, real estate and multi-level marketing. In the career of financial planning, however, there still seems to be a work style perception that is not as attractive to women as it is to men. The perception (be it real or perceived) of sacrificing half of your life (mainly your family life) in order to have a successful career is a turn-off for many women. The demands of caring for family and developing a successful practice in the financial planning world create so much stress for women that this work/life imbalance becomes a negative factor when deciding to pursue this career.

In a June 2015 article titled, "3 Ways to Close the Gender Gap Among Advisors" Erinn Ford, President of Cetera Advisors, recounts the story of two women she observed very early on in their financial careers. Both seemed to have what it takes to be successful advisors and both were working for similarly large firms. Years later, when the author crossed paths with both women once again, she noticed that one woman had become an independent financial advisor, had built a thriving practice, and was looking to buy another practice as well. The other woman had never left her junior role and was considering leaving the industry. Ford remarked, "the one who advanced as an advisor repeatedly stressed the benefits of being coached by advisors within her practice on building a book of business and balancing that with her desire to raise a family. On the other hand, the woman who ultimately left the industry said, "I felt like I needed to choose between having a family and trying to move up in this business." Clearly, when a woman believes she can have both a work and family life, and when she seeks mentors who affirm this belief, she is less apt to abandon her career goals.

Recently, the Practice Management Group of State Street Global Advisors and *InvestmentNews Research* collaborated to produce a study called "Women in Advice: Inspiring the Next Generation of Financial Advisors." The study was designed both to draw more attention to the issues facing women advisors and, more importantly, to initiate change. After surveying 612 male and female advisors, the responses showed that work, life, and family balance remains the number one reason women don't seek advancement in the industry. This report overlaps with the fact that the number of women CFP® professionals has hovered at 23% since 2003 and that in 2017 only 21.4% of lead advisors in independent firms were female. You may be surprised to know that this report also noted that work, life, and family balance has now become a man's issue as well.

This comprehensive research confirms as well what we heard from our interviewees regarding this topic. The women advisors we spoke to all had opinions when the subject of work/life balance arose. It became obvious that the quality of one's support network and the expectations and/or perceived expectations of a firm played a large role in the pressure women advisors feel when it comes to work/life balance. Take a look at their insights and see if anything sounds familiar to you.

- "It's very hard work – very hard to juggle kids and a job. I made it because I had to. I had no one supporting me. I worked 80 hours per week and had an office at home that I used a lot. I was there when my kids got home from school and then continued to work after they went to bed."

- "Work/life balance is a big issue. I feel like my first job is taking care of my clients, my second job is taking care of my kids, and my third job is taking care of my home. Women can't make it to events comfortably in the evenings or weekends. It's very difficult, especially if you want to be a rainmaker. Some will do this part-time to make it work. I almost wanted to forget it and go teach instead!"

- "It's hard … the job requires tough skin."

- "Intestinal fortitude … women have it everywhere, they don't want it at work."

- "It's not a 9 to 5 job."

- "Work/life balance is hard. It's very hard to find time with your family."

- "I worked my ass off to support myself!"

- "As an independent, at least I can choose the 80 hours I work each week."

- "As a working mom – balance was hard to put family first while maintaining a professional career."

- "I identify with my role in this professional space, but I want to succeed there as well as being a mom, wife, daughter, etc."

- "I would NOT get into the industry now."

- "If you have kids, it's harder to start. Without kids is easier."

- "There are unwritten expectations. A man I worked with works 5 am-9 pm and Saturdays 9-4 and "they" say he is successful. He has no kids but has a new condo. It's just not the same as having kids to pay for and be with. NO BALANCE."

Through our coaching, we have seen how our clients – both male and female advisors – have experienced work, life, and family balance issues. It's apparent to us and to many other specialists, that the financial profession would gain tremendously by lightening the demands and expectations on advisors in order to create a more balanced environment that supports and nurtures the true needs of the women and men who choose to make this a career.

Sexual Harassment

The *#MeToo* movement that began in late 2017 imposed a magnifying glass on a nearly invisible epidemic of sexual harassment against women across all walks of life and throughout various industries. Prominent and powerful men have been called on the carpet for behavior that until now has long been ignored, hushed, and/or silenced with millions of dollars.

In March 2018, Andrew Welsch wrote an article for *Financial-Planning.com* to address the issue of sexual harassment in wealth management. The article contains a *SourceMedia Research* survey that includes responses on sexual harassment from 3,000 individuals across a wide range of professions. Notably, when it came to sexual misconduct, the wealth management industry was pinpointed as the worst. One-third of the women in the study who were in wealth management reported a high prevalence of sexual misconduct in the workplace. Another 22% said the harassment is moderate. One in three women said that they have personally experienced unwelcome sexual misconduct in the workplace, such as inappropriate questions or comments, demeaning nicknames, jokes, innuendos, and even retaliation.

Men and women often see things differently. Thus, in many cases, the simple definition or explanation of sexual harassment may be different between the genders. This disparity led one female advisor to say: "I think the men just don't know what's appropriate and what's not appropriate." In this *SourceMedia Research* study, 54% of women claim there is a need for increased sensitivity training compared to 32% of men. And 73% of women reported a need to change workplace culture compared to 54% of men.

Not surprisingly, the permeating attitude of male dominance in wealth management extends beyond the walls of individual firms. For example, in 2017 there was an incident in New York's financial district that went viral on social media. As part of a campaign to encourage more companies to add women to their boards, State Street Global Advisors placed what became known as The Fearless Girl statue in front of Wall Street's iconic Charging Bull. The Fearless Girl sculpture gained national recognition as an empowering image for women. Within a few short days, however, a photo of a young man in a suit appearing to be sexually engaged with the girl statue went viral. What message does this photographic insult send to women and girls around the country? What's on the welcome mat for women on Wall Street?

Amazingly, despite the external and internal barriers that are stacked up against you, women continue to succeed! Our plan for this book and for our coaching and speaking commitments is to help even more women succeed. Of course, we can't tackle and solve the issues of an industry in a single book. However, we can equip and empower more women like you to flourish in a male-dominated industry. It's been shown over and over that women make exceptional financial advisors. There are natural qualities that women possess that position them to organically align with client needs and desires.

We want you to embrace your womanhood and lead your practice *A Woman's Way*.

Section two highlights some of the special strengths women possess that seem custom-made to meet what clients seek in their financial advisor.

We believe you'll see yourself in the mirror.

SECTION 2

Lead with Authenticity

"Authenticity is about the choice to show up and be real. The choice to be honest. The choice to let our true selves be seen."
- Brené Brown

You've already got what it takes

Women make great advisors. They inherently have certain natural qualities and characteristics that perfectly align with the profession of financial planning. The prospects who seek out and hire a financial planner want certain features in the person they engage. Beyond results and ethical behavior, they want to be heard and understood. They want to understand their finances and not have their advisor talk over their heads. They need to be assured that their advisor is acting in their best interest at all times. They want a relationship rather than feeling like a number in a system.

A June 2015 article posted by Rick Kahler on *Time Inc.* titled, "Four Qualities a Financial Advisor Ought to Have" highlighted a 2014 study by the Financial Planning Association's Research and Practice Institute. This study determined that nearly 90% of clients want their financial advisor to be a strong leader. While this claim alone was not surprising, the client description of "leadership" (as you will see) took on new meaning – a meaning that we think demonstrates why more women are needed in the industry. What's more, the results of this study make clear why leadership is such a dominant thread running through this book.

Clients from this study reported that good leaders (i.e. their advisors) should have four dominant qualities: expertise, skill as a guide, deep understanding, and vulnerability. Let's look at each of these traits to see how you can (and often already do) embody them.

Expertise

Clients are definitely looking for a certain level of expertise from their financial advisor. This really shouldn't come as a surprise. When clients make the decision to engage a financial advisor, they put a very high level of trust in believing that the advisor knows her or his stuff.

There is no question that general training and ongoing professional learning and development for financial advisors help to guarantee a certain level of expertise. However, the training and preparation vary greatly outside of the Certified Financial Planner™ or CFP® designation, and the public is often instructed to look for the CFP® designation when searching for an advisor. In a *Forbes.com* January 2017 article by Roger Ma, Mr. Ma suggests that his readers, "Try to glean what steps an advisor has taken to continue to increase their knowledge base in personal finance. One way to gauge this is through the various certifications they may hold." Ma states that the CFP® designation is often considered "the gold standard" within the profession and suggests that people research potential advisors' educational background, experience, website, planning processes, additional qualifications, as well their thought processes before making a selection.

Only 23% of female financial advisors are CFP® certified. This number has remained the same for over 10 years. Perhaps women who are trying to balance a home life while building a solid book of business struggle to find the space, energy, and alone time needed to engage in the process of intensive studying required for the CFP® exams. The fact remains that some clients (and advisors) are drawn to the CFP® designation while others are not. We know plenty of very successful, well-loved financial advisors who do not have the CFP® designation and an equal number who do.

The fact remains that clients want expertise and they may research you in order to find what they're looking for or confirm what they've been told about you. Knowing this, ensure that your expertise and knowledge are adequately portrayed on your website and in your bios. Be sure to list any and all certifications you possess, such as the CFP®, CDFA®, CFA, and ChFA to name a few. Clearly articulate any specialty areas in all forms of marketing. For example, be sure to highlight your expertise when writing articles and in your LinkedIn profile, too.

We certainly understand that women sometimes struggle with promoting or sharing their expertise. However, knowing that this is one thing that's important to your prospects, learn to toot your own horn. Think of it this way; informing your prospects about your expertise is giving them what they want. And if you don't tell them, they may never find out.

What other qualities do clients look for in their financial advisor? Let's expand on three additional dominant qualities from Rick Kahler that fall into the "soft skills" category.

Skills as a Guide

As a noun in the Merriam-Webster Dictionary, the word "guide" refers to a person who advises or shows the way to others or directs a person's conduct or course of life. It could also refer to a thing that helps someone form an opinion or decision. As a verb, guide means to direct or have influence on the course of action of someone or something.

By these definitions, it's obvious to see how the term guide can be associated with a financial advisor. In many ways, guides keep people safe. They know where the dangers lurk, and they are informed on how to handle and cope with uncertainties. They are trained to stay calm in anxious situations and to provide a sense of comfort to those relying on their skills. When considering the volatility of the market and all the factors not within the control of financial advisors, their ability to stay calm while guiding clients becomes highly important.

Both genders have their preferred ways of coping with stress. A *HuffingtonPost.com* article titled, "How men and women handle stress differently" by Dr. Gail Gross pointed out several key factors that give women advisors an edge when dealing with stress. Some of these differences are rooted in three hormones: cortisol, epinephrine and oxytocin. Cortisol and epinephrine are primarily triggered to raise our blood pressure. Oxytocin is triggered to soften the reaction produced by cortisol and epinephrine. Men typically produce less oxytocin than women, giving them a stronger reaction to cortisol and epinephrine. The estrogen hormone in women also increases their drive to protect others, especially their relationships.

Relationships are so important to women that their self-esteem can be directly impacted by the success of their relationships. Men, on the other hand, tend to be more invested in performance and competition.

According to Dr. Gross, men are often not tuned into social cues as well as women. For example, evidence shows that women can pick up six different facial cues whereas men pick up one in similar circumstances. When acting as a guide for your clients, it often becomes necessary to hear what's not being said, and women are better able to tune into those cues.

While it's not uncommon for women to internalize their stress, they seek outlets of support, such as girlfriends, sisters, and mentors, to lighten their discomfort. Unlike women, "Men seek to escape when confronted by stress. As problem solvers, they compartmentalize and repress their feelings to either fight or run away. They may even change the subject through diversions," according to Dr. Gross.

If you're a mom, **you've seen it all**. You've probably handled more stress than you care to remember. If you're a caregiver to an aging parent, you've most likely been managing the situation from the beginning because that's what women do. As a female advisor, your abilities to stay calm under pressure while tending and befriending help you to establish that trusting relationship with your clients. When the market goes crazy, many of your clients will need reassurance. Some will need hand-holding. Some will need to be talked off the market ledge. The kind of clients that are attracted to you will welcome your kind words and reassuring voice when their world is turning upside down. This comes naturally to you because you're practiced at it from all the other elements of your life.

Deep Understanding

The third quality that clients seek in their advisors is **deep understanding**. Many of the women in our survey expressed that women advisors simply "go deeper" with their clients than most men do. Here are some of their comments to the question: "What do you think makes a woman successful as an advisor?"

- "Women have an ability to relate and build deeper relationships beyond business."

- "Women have the ability to understand their client."

- "Women have a willingness to spend quality time with their clients."

- "Women have a higher emotional intelligence quotient. Good empathizers can relate, especially to other women."

- "Women get personal."

- "In the boy's club, it's all about sales."

- "Women talk less about the market and are more client-focused."
- "Women are better educators and value education more than men."

- "Women are able to be more empathetic than men."

- "Women have a way of being more straightforward with the hard information. Men are harsher and more clinical (not comfortable going to the emotional part)."

Many of the qualities that are embedded in the meaning of "deep understanding" are words that our survey group identified to describe themselves, their skills, and other female advisors. Words such as listening, empathy, openness, collaboration, heart, compassion, curiosity, intuition, communication, creativity, authenticity, and relationship building.

Do these words embody you too? **These words reflect *A Woman's Way* of doing business as a female financial advisor.** When you embrace these words, you allow yourself to authentically connect with and serve current clients, attract new clients, and grow your practice. And then you can truly say you're growing and managing your practice *A Woman's Way*.

In the upcoming sections, we will highlight specific strategies and techniques that are in direct alignment with these female qualities to help you grow and manage yourself and your practice in a way that's not only comfortable for you but proven to be successful.

Vulnerability

Kahler's last quality that clients seek in their advisor is **vulnerability**. We're pretty certain that if you asked a room full of financial advisors how they feel about vulnerability, the answer might not come back very positive. Feeling vulnerable is generally uncomfortable, and for some, being vulnerable in front of clients can be incredibly uncomfortable. Sometimes there's a sense that allowing yourself to appear vulnerable may cause clients to question your expertise.

The successful women advisors we've coached and queried all agree that not being afraid to admit to your client when you don't know something is important to building trust. Clients appreciate when you admit you're not perfect. It makes you human. It puts you more on the client's level and is appealing especially for those clients who find it hard to talk to their advisors for fear of feeling stupid.

Being vulnerable helps you to connect with others. In our experience, it appears that the vast majority of women are more willing to show their vulnerability to clients than men. However, women tend to be very guarded about showing their vulnerability to their male counterparts for fear of criticism and judgment.

When you consider these four dominant qualities that clients seek in their financial advisor – expertise, skill as a guide, deep understanding, and vulnerability – it's obvious that women already possess the qualities necessary to become thriving financial advisors. For many women, they naturally enjoy the qualities that clients are looking for in an advisor. We see these assets every day, but the problem is, women often get in their own way. What's worse is that often times, they don't even know it. As coaches, we are very familiar with these self-sabotaging behaviors, beliefs, and thoughts as well.

It's important to overcome your INTERNAL barriers, all the thoughts, beliefs and actions that stop you from making progress and being as productive as you possibly can be. Sometimes your internal barriers become so tall that you feel as though they are mountains you can't cross.

Over the years, we've probably met just about all of your internal barriers at one time or another. We feel confident in how to guide you as you climb over the mountains, and we know what equipment you'll need to be successful. As we move forward, we'll introduce you to the most familiar internal barriers (no doubt, you will already know many by name). Simultaneously, we'll give you the tools you'll need to remove each barrier and replace it with new leadership skills to better lead yourself, your productivity and your relationships.

Section Three will focus on the internal barriers that impact your overall productivity with life and work. For example, we'll address your internal perfectionist, procrastinator, delegator, and multi-tasker. We'll tackle your time management struggles, attention management challenges, and how you make choices as you deal with clutter, interruptions and email. Overcoming all of these barriers will require strong leadership skills to lead yourself towards noticeably greater success and improved work/life balance.

Section Four will focus on those interior barriers that create obstacles to growing your practice. These are the beliefs, thoughts, and actions that prevent you from doing what needs to be done to bring on more business in a productive and proactive manner. We'll address your tendency to avoid asking for referrals, asking for help, and settling for COI relationships that are unproductive. We'll dive deep into why you lower your expectations and don't fully trust the relationships that surround you. Strengthening your leadership skills in the area of leading your relationships will enable your practice to grow exponentially. *A Woman's Way* practice grows in profitability the more it is in alignment with who you are personally and authentically.

There's a strong chance that as you read about these personal internal barriers you face as a woman and as a woman financial advisor, you'll see or hear yourself loud and clear. You may have already crashed through some of these barriers and have them well under control, yet others remain solid and completely out of control. The reality is that all of these obstacles can be turned around to drastically improve your overall productivity in life and in your practice or firm.

Leading oneself and leading your relationships will become the pathway to climb your mountain. We will support your natural talents, skills, and characteristics by empowering the leader within you to grow and manage a financial practice YOUR way – *A Woman's Way*. Of course, if you struggle to hold yourself accountable while applying the tactics for leading yourself or leading your relationships, please know that we are just a phone call or email away.

Are you ready to crash through some barriers?

SECTION 3

Lead Your Productivity

"It is not the mountain we conquer but ourselves."
– Sir Edmund Hillary

Do you ever feel out of control before your first sip of coffee? Being unproductive is frustrating and feels bad, especially when you know that you can do better AND you know what to do but you're simply not doing it. Why is this? The most likely reason is that you probably haven't taken the time to assess what is working and what is not.

We know what it's like. It's so easy to get caught up in the rat race, running through your groundhog days so fast that you are not really living but merely surviving. Our fast-paced, high-tech culture can make anyone feel crazy and off-balance, kind of like you're on a hamster wheel. But what if you could begin to make more conscious choices about how you want your life to be? Yes, there is hope! In all the craziness, one of the things you are likely missing is the availability of effective, intuitive systems that will work for and with you.

A great way to start paying a new kind of attention is to take a few minutes to closely look around your office. Make a note of what's working. For instance, if your filing system is convenient, organized and makes it easy to access what you need when you need it and it works for you as it is, add that system to your list. This review of your personal space helps so you can build on good systems that you already have in place that work for you.

On the flip side, it's crucial to recognize what is failing miserably. Where do you notice that you start to spiral out of control? If you can't think of anywhere off the top of your head, we'll help you out. This section contains common internal barriers that female financial advisors struggle with and provides you with solutions. If you lead yourself to remove even one of the barriers itemized below, chances are that you will experience a positive impact on your life and work.

- Work/life balance

- Taking care of you

- Perfectionism

- Delegation

- Multitasking

- Email

- Your time

- Interruptions

- Choices

Since we've already established that you have the qualities and characteristics that clients seek in a financial advisor (expertise, skill as a guide, deep understanding, and vulnerability), why not leverage those qualities to productively manage yourself and your practice? Just as you are a guide for your clients, allow us to guide you through creating *A Woman's Way* financial practice and empower you to overcome your internal barriers.

Take a deep breath, open your airways and all your senses, and allow your true inner person to reach for a level of productivity balance that you never thought possible. Let's start with the elusive work/life balance.

Lead your work/life balance

While some say there is no such thing as life balance, countless people still seek it. For many, internal barriers to achieving a sense of balance in life are huge!

Balance is a funny thing. Balance is a state you can achieve for a bit (a minute, maybe a few days, or even a week), but staying there for any sustained period of time seems virtually impossible. The best way to discover your secret to balance is to be keenly aware of what balance looks like to you. Once you have a vision of your life in balance, you can strive to achieve it. It can be done, but you absolutely must create a plan for when life gets crazy and knocks you out of balance again. And we guarantee you will be knocked out of balance over and over again, so don't forget, maintaining balance is just as important as achieving it.

The people you ask to describe their vision of balance will likely each have a very different answer because we all have different components, parts, and priorities in our lives. Of course, there may be some common threads to what life balance can mean, but because our individual lives resemble a kaleidoscope, we each have different pieces that make up who we are. Some of these pieces might include having a spouse, a significant other, kids, pets, aging parents, a house, a second home, kids in college, high-maintenance clients, an unprofessional business partner, work travel, an empty nest, an unreliable car, a long commute, a special needs child, kids who play intense sports – you get the idea. If you add the words "or not" after each of the above pieces, you can see the multitude of combinations that life can take on to make your kaleidoscope image truly and uniquely yours. In fact, our own different components make up the thing we each call "my life."

Knowing that this list can go on forever, check off all the kaleidoscope pieces that apply to you and feel free to add more.

- ☐ Income earner
- ☐ Breadwinner
- ☐ Boss
- ☐ Employee
- ☐ Partner
- ☐ Business Owner
- ☐ Manager
- ☐ Spouse
- ☐ Significant other
- ☐ Mom
- ☐ Sister
- ☐ Daughter
- ☐ Aunt
- ☐ Niece
- ☐ Grandmother
- ☐ Parent caretaker
- ☐ Bill payer
- ☐ Money manager
- ☐ Grocery shopper
- ☐ Clothes shopper
- ☐ Carpool driver
- ☐ Sports mom
- ☐ Dance mom
- ☐ Band mom
- ☐ Piano mom
- ☐ Karate mom
- ☐ PTA mom
- ☐ Band mom

- ☐ Breakfast chef
- ☐ Lunch chef
- ☐ Dinner chef
- ☐ Dishwasher
- ☐ Dishwasher loader
- ☐ Dishwasher emptier
- ☐ Laundry doer
- ☐ Boo-boo kisser
- ☐ Snow-shoveler
- ☐ Household manager
- ☐ Referee
- ☐ Judge
- ☐ Jury
- ☐ Traveler
- ☐ Board member
- ☐ Committee member
- ☐ Neighbor
- ☐ Friend
- ☐ Dry cleaning picker-upper
- ☐ Homework supervisor
- ☐ _____
- ☐ _____
- ☐ _____
- ☐ _____
- ☐ _____

Take a look at all the pieces that make up your life right now. And then "POOF!!" Just when you think you have it all figured out, something changes. You get married, find out you're pregnant, you learn that your mom fell and broke her hip, you land a new HUGE client, a client passes away, your child is heading to college, you are elected president of your association, you get divorced, you change jobs, your significant other loses a job, and the life list literally goes on and on. How is someone supposed to find balance among all this chaos and change? Well, it isn't easy but it is possible. You must want balance and be willing to be flexible. You must become the leading lady of your life and learn to lead the pieces that are within your control…both in your life and in your practice.

> *"Change is the only constant in life."*
> *- The Greek philosopher, Heraclitus*

First, accept some universal truths. "Change is the only constant in life" is one of these truths. The real secret to life balance is understanding that the earlier in your life you can accept the constancy of change, the easier your life will be. If you have already taken this truth to heart, you may have noticed that you already roll more easily with these changes because you have come to expect the unexpected. Of course, many of us hear this saying but do not take in its meaning. This response is so typical that we urge you to take some time to reflect on this saying – Change is the only constant in life – right now so you can fully absorb its meaning into your belief system. Accepting this truth is a great step towards living on an entirely higher and different level of thinking and believing. Knowing that change is constant makes you stronger; accepting the fluid nature of reality assures you that you are ready to take on anything.

Taking this truth one step further leads to the recognition that change happens during good as well as bad times. Thus, just when you think you've hit rock bottom, things usually change for the better. On the other side, though, just when you think things are running smoothly and nothing can go wrong, something usually does. It's the nature of the beast.

"This too shall pass."

"This too shall pass" is a sister to the universal truth "Change is the only constant in life." Like the inevitability of change, "This too shall pass" is true in both good times and bad. How do you know this? Look back on any part of your life that was amazing or unbearable. Neither lasted forever and here you are now. Are the extreme ups and downs hard? You bet! But whatever it is, this too shall pass.

ACTION

Write both of these universal truths on a piece of paper or sticky note, put them in a place that you'll see every day (on your mirror, computer monitor, refrigerator), and read them daily until you "get them." One of our friends loves to use mirror markers so she can write motivating statements like these right on her bedroom and bathroom mirrors!

The following sections are designed to help you gain the ever-elusive work/life balance you seek. Each suggestion plays a significant role in not only getting you into balance but also working to keep you there. Your commitment to yourself and your willingness to lead these efforts will help you attain your goal of balance.

Now…get ready to unleash the leader within you!

Lead yourself first

How often do you tend to the needs of others before tending to your own needs? We get it. However, you can't let "being a woman" become an excuse for not tending to your own personal needs and values. Most women we know usually ignore their needs and values while focusing on others. In fact, you might be asking yourself, "How can I be ignoring my needs and values when I don't even know what they are?"

This is exactly our point. Do you know what you **need** to make life work best for you? Do you know the core **values** that drive who you are and the decisions you make on a daily basis? If not, we're going to fix that. Not knowing core needs and values about yourself creates an internal barrier that you don't even know exists. It builds a wall between feeling balanced and feeling completely out of alignment.

What do you think we mean by "lead yourself first?" It's kind of like the oxygen mask in the airplane. You're told to put your own mask on first and then assist your child because if you don't take care of yourself first, you can't be there for your child. The same applies to your practice. If you don't take good care of yourself first, you can't take good care of your clients or your practice.

As women, there are many areas of our lives that need our attention. When even one of these pieces is neglected, you know it; you can feel it permeating through your skin. For example, when there is a lack of family time, an issue at work, trouble carving out "me" time, health issues, weight gain, or money problems, you tend to feel out of sorts. Any of these can cause you enough worry to lose sleep. In turn, lack of sleep makes you feel grumpier and your issues don't get the necessary attention to make them go away. Now the pieces of your life that are being ignored seem to grow in your head, appearing worse than they really are, and the preoccupations of your mental and emotional energies create a lack of productivity that can make you question the reason you get out of bed every morning.

When you find yourself in a place of discontent and it feels like you are in a downward spiral, you're probably out of alignment with what most matters to you on the inside. Something feels off and that "off" feeling can present itself in many ways. You might get that bad feeling in the pit of your stomach, but you can't quite put your finger on what it is that's bothering you. Or you get neck pain from stress you can't name. If you begin to pay attention to your body, it will tell you what signal it sends to tell you something is "off."

Begin by taking a look around. If nothing bad has happened at work, if the kids are doing well, if you had a nice dinner last night with your partner, and you can't think of a thing that is wrong, yet you still feel "off," you need to step back and realize that there is something at work here that goes deeper than your daily life. Your inner guidance system is sending you a red flag.

Your job is to pay attention to that flag and address it. This inner guidance system is also known as your *needs and values system*. When you are out of alignment with what makes life work for you and what you stand for, you find yourself in a bad place for no *apparent* reason. For example, as a female financial advisor, you most likely have had male role models, educators, and mentors. They probably taught you their successful ways of bringing in new business. Sometimes, the way that works for them doesn't feel quite right for you. In your head, you know their methods have worked for them but something inside your gut is telling you that it's not the right system for you. Yet you can't quite put your finger on why. There's a red flag that needs your attention. At that moment, your inner guidance system is on fire!

If you've never done the work to determine the true needs and values that act as a compass for your life, now's the time. Without knowing this information, it's very easy to make decisions that disrupt your fulfillment and happiness, not just at work but at home as well. Our role as coaches is to help our clients set the stage for what matters most, to help them understand where their attention should and/or needs to be and to know how to stay hyper-focused to maintain alignment at all times.

ACTION

To clarify exactly what you need and value in your life, let's take a look at the following exercise. Don't overthink it. Respond with your heart and soul, not with your head. This is not about what you think someone else wants to hear.

NEEDS tend to be personal priorities and principles, and until your NEEDS are met, life doesn't "work."

Selecting from the following list, what are your top three needs?

☐	Achievement	☐	Love
☐	Adventure	☐	Nature
☐	Aesthetic	☐	Peace
☐	Community	☐	Pleasure
☐	Equality	☐	Power
☐	Fame	☐	Self-Worth
☐	Family	☐	Service
☐	Freedom	☐	Spirituality
☐	Fellowship	☐	Wealth
☐	Happiness	☐	Wisdom
☐	Health		

Write your needs here.

Needs _____

   _____

   _____

VALUES tend to be personal qualities or passions. They are what you stand for or who you are.

Selecting from the following list, what are your top three values?

☐ Accountability	☐ Forgiveness
☐ Affection	☐ Honesty
☐ Autonomy	☐ Humor
☐ Competency	☐ Knowledge
☐ Courage	☐ Loyalty
☐ Courtesy	☐ Obedience
☐ Creative	☐ Order
☐ Discipline	☐ Reason
☐ Drive	☐ Service
☐ Fairness	☐ Tolerance
☐ Flexibility	

Write your values here.

Values _____

   _____

   _____

You may have found this exercise to be extremely easy or you may have struggled with it. It's OK because either way you now know what steers you and you can easily pinpoint what is not working at any given moment. With this information, you can now make a correction to bring yourself back into alignment. It is good to have a sense of what works for you. But it is great to have the actual, concrete words to define what works for you and be able to fall back on these qualities when you are out of sync with what makes you *YOU*.

Picture your coffee pot at home. Not the Keurig kind but the one that uses a filter. If you were to put coffee grounds in the pot without the filter, you would get quite a mess in your coffee pot, right? When you use the filter, you get what you want and need--a great cup of coffee. Your needs and values act like a coffee filter. They only let the good stuff come through so you get what you need and value – a balanced home and work life that stays in alignment without the mess.

Let's look at a specific example. Let's say that one of your needs is NATURE, and, as we have said, until your needs are met, life simply won't "work." If you look at your schedule and every waking minute is spent in one cave or another (home, car, or work) and you're not allowing yourself to be outside in nature, you will be feeling an imbalance and may not even know why. What correction can you make? Well, you can take a walk first thing in the morning or take a walk at lunchtime. Getting yourself outside will feed your inner guidance system and restore balance.

Another example could be that you value HONESTY and work for a firm that just doesn't feel like it fits you any longer. All of a sudden, you put two and two together and remember those incidents when a client's best interest did not take priority. You feel out of alignment. Perhaps it's time you make a change and follow your value of honesty by confronting and resolving the issues or leaving this firm in order to practice as a fiduciary. Either way, you are aligning with your values.

Staying focused on your needs and values will hold you steady when things feel off kilter. Remember to pay attention and heed your *intuition*. That's one of your greatest strengths as a woman; use it every day. We recommend posting your identified needs and values where you can see them daily to keep you centered. We also recommend that you use your needs and values to guide your decisions moving forward. We'll be sure to point out the importance of this practice again from time to time.

Lead your perfectionist and delegator

Perfectionism is a blessing and a curse. We feel so good about ourselves because we can do it all (we think better than anyone else) – and we do end up doing it all. However, we become our own worst enemy by insisting on doing everything, and we end up getting in our own way.

> *Just because you CAN do something*
> *doesn't mean you should.*

Perfectionism and delegation are like oil and water. They simply don't mix, so until you work on getting your perfectionistic tendencies under control, your delegator will remain dormant.

The core problem is that we've smothered our delegator by convincing ourselves that there is nobody else to do a job like we can. Sometimes what we really mean is that we don't trust anyone else to do it 'right,' as if we hold the magical power of doing every job right. But is this really true?

The first excuse that comes out of a perfectionist's mouth is this: "If I want it done right, I'll have to do it myself. By the time I explain it to the other person, I may as well do it myself." Sound familiar? Thought so. We'd like you to meet perfectionism, yet another internal barrier that blocks your productivity.

Our culture influences women to feel the need to be perfect. Most women we talk to who call themselves perfectionists really don't want to be this way, but they feel that they have to be. Here's a little secret: *perfection is not attainable.*

In the Amish culture, they believe that only God is perfect. To demonstrate this belief, in every handmade quilt they purposely make a mistake somewhere to remind them that nothing on earth is perfect. Striving for perfection can bring about depression, anxiety, stress, feelings of hopelessness, loss of interest, loss of appetite, and it has even been known to lead to nervous breakdowns. Perfectionism will ultimately get in your way. It will slow down your road to success in a big way.

According to *The Confidence Code* by Katty Kay and Claire Shipman, perfectionism is also a confidence killer. As a financial advisor, sometimes the quest for perfection inhibits your ability to make decisions, especially those that must be made quickly. Perfectionism holds you back. It stops you from taking risks and slows down your progress as you continually try to get things 'just right' to avoid judgment or failure.

The Confidence Code also reveals that success correlates more closely with **confidence** than with **competence**, meaning that in order to succeed it's more important to be confident than it is to be competent. (Maybe you need to read that last sentence again!) And because perfectionism tends to kill confidence, women who lack confidence may struggle to get ahead. No doubt you are as alarmed by this revelation as we were when we first read it.

The sad truth is, as a perfectionist, you are not magical — that's just a big bunch of bologna. You're simply being a stubborn, controlling perfectionist. Yes, you. We recognize this because we are recovering perfectionists ourselves! We can look in the mirror and see ourselves saying those exact words at one point in our lives and believing every word. Can we do it all? Yes. Do we need to do it all? No.

Here's the key – stop self-sabotaging your productivity and empower other people to do the things you don't need to do or shouldn't be doing. In other words, silence your perfectionist and empower your delegator.

There are many capable people in the world who can learn quickly and perform the heroic tasks that you deem impossible for another human to learn or complete. Perhaps this is a universal truth that should be written on your mirror:

"I am not perfect and others can do what I can do."

The faster you understand this truth and BELIEVE it, the better your life and your practice will become. Free yourself to focus on what you do best to ensure that your practice grows, that your clients are serviced well, and that your confidence never gets impaired by perfectionism. Here's an exercise that will enlighten you, potentially lighten your load, and move you past your perfectionist barrier to release and embolden your delegator once and for all.

ACTION

Stop, Start and Continue Exercise

One of Patty's favorite productivity tools that she introduces to her clients is a great exercise called Stop, Start and Continue. First, get a piece of paper and turn it sideways. Draw 2 lines to make 3 columns. Label the first column STOP, the second column START and the third column CONTINUE. Take a minute right now and write down all the things that you know you should

STOP doing. This list should include all the things that are stealing your productivity away from what you need to be doing. Be sure to cross the barriers separating your personal life from your business life and include items from both sides. List the specific activities that someone else could and should be doing or that you do that don't serve you well.

STOP	START	CONTINUE

Now create a second list to include all the actions you need to START doing. This list will enlighten you. Perhaps you need to start delegating more, start your day with a walk, start getting home earlier, start using a single calendar, start eating better, you name it.

Finally, create a third list of all the things you need to CONTINUE doing. If something is working, by all means, continue doing it. If you enjoy doing something so much that you hate to give it up, continue doing it.

Be sure to run all the items on your lists through your new favorite filters – your needs and values. Focus on staying in alignment. By the end of this exercise, you will have direction. Then it's time to ACT. Choose where you will begin and take baby steps towards letting nonproductive activities go and starting new behaviors.

Now, let's all raise our glass in a toast to say, "Nobody is perfect...not even me!"

Lead your multitasker

Or maybe that should say LEAVE your multitasker.

Does this describe you? You're sitting at your desk eating your lunch, checking your email, finalizing your quarterly market analysis, texting your mom about her doctor's appointment and listening to a webinar on the impact of the new tax laws. Wow! Did you know that multitasking is an internal barrier that causes you to lose 40% of your productivity? Yikes! And you thought you were being efficient! Sorry, you're not.

The good news is that women are good at juggling. The bad news is that women are good at juggling!

Women think they're great at multitasking because we do it everywhere all the time. How else would we get things done? How many tasks or projects can you juggle at one time? How many people can you give attention to at the same time? Multitasking has become an epidemic and it's not good for you or your practice. In reality, it's a massive internal barrier to accomplishing more of what you want in your day.

In an article posted on *Psychology Today*, Susan Weinschenk PhD shared some alarming statistics related to what she prefers to call "task switching." She believes that multitaskers are actually task switchers because they switch from task to task quickly. Research proves that we actually can't do two things at once and do them well. Look at how well people can walk on the street and text on their cell phones! Not so much. Check out what research has to say about these task switching facts:

- It takes more time to get tasks completed if you switch between them than if you do them one at a time.

- You make more errors when you switch than if you do one task at a time. If the tasks are complex, then these time and error penalties increase.

- Each task switch might waste only 1/10th of a second, but if you do a lot of switching in a day it can add up to a loss of 40% of your productivity.

Task switching involves several parts of your brain. Brain scans conducted during task switching show activity in four major area and here's how they break down:

The **pre-frontal cortex** is involved in shifting and focusing your attention and selecting which task to do when.

The **posterior parietal lobe** activates rules for each task you switch to.

The **anterior cingulate gyrus** monitors errors.

The **pre-motor cortex** is preparing for you to move in some way.

That's a lot of activity and greatly impacts attention management, making multitasking or task switching unhealthy. Stanford researchers also proved that those who try to do more than one thing at a time are far less productive than those who stay focused on one task at a time.

The Stanford study shows that people who are regularly bombarded with several streams of electronic information do not pay attention. In addition, they can't control their memory or switch from one job to another as well as those who prefer to complete one task at a time. The lead author of this study said, "We kept looking for what they're better at and we didn't find it." These researchers suggested that multi-taskers are slowed down significantly by irrelevant information.

So many of our female financial advisor clients try to tell us that they are SO productive because they can multitask. However, as the research has proven, the sad truth is that multitaskers are paying a big mental price. Being busy does not necessarily equate to being effective or productive. In fact, everything becomes a distraction for the multitasker because a task switcher's brain is trained to jump from one thing to another constantly. Therefore, there tends to be no priority on what they jump to next. We could actually accomplish more by doing less.

How do you lead your multitasker or task switcher? Imagine if you could gain back 40% of your productivity! This possibility alone should be enough motivation to try a few new things.

Here are a few extra tips from Susan Weinschenk, PhD:

1.   Practice the 80/20 rule. Focus on the 20% of your tasks that really are effective and do them one at a time.

2.   Practice "batch processing." This process works for processing email, checking voicemail, returning phone calls, etc. Pick a time of day (or a couple of times) for when you will take care of these tasks and don't allow yourself to go there until that time. This might require that you train your team and even your clients to know when you will be addressing these chores to minimize distractions.

3.   Work on your most important task first. Once those more important things are done, you can move on to other less important ones.

4.   Use concentrated times. Block out a chunk of time to complete one task. Turn off all distractions. Close your door if needed and focus your attention.

5.   Leave blank space in your calendar to rest your brain. You will actually get more done if you allow your brain to rest and integrate information. Perhaps leaving time at lunch to walk outside is the perfect remedy for your brain.

ACTION

Which of these tips can you adopt into your day and begin doing to lead your multitasker to regain some productivity? Initiate a conversation with your team about how they can manage things while you're engaged in your 'focus' time. Maybe you can think of another advisor you know or one of your COIs who could work on these behaviors with you. Call her. Ask if she would like to work together as accountability partners as each of you pursues regaining control of your productivity. Together you can offer support and maybe even take that lunchtime walk together.

Lead your email

Do you lead your email or does your email lead you?

When email leads you, it looks like this:

> The first thing you do in the morning is open your email. You're checking your email at breakfast. You're checking email at a red light. You're deep into email at your desk shortly after you sit down. Before you realize it, an hour of your day has evaporated. You react instantly to the "you've got mail" ding, whistle, or beep on your phone.

Sound familiar? This seemingly small internal barrier of not wanting to miss something, believing that every email of life or death importance, that people expect an instant reply or holding on to every email to infinity continually disrupts your productivity.

Love it or hate it, email is here to stay so you might want to take some time now to get a grip on it. So often, our clients tell us they have thousands of emails in their inbox but it works for them. They say it doesn't bother them to have that many there because then they at least know they can find something. Does it really work to have thousands of emails in your inbox? It might until something falls through the cracks. Something really important. Then panic sets in and excuses begin.

Email is a vital part of our communication in business, so it stands to reason that we should learn how to use it properly. The number one thing to know about email is the difference between **checking email** and **processing email**. We all check our email a thousand times a day – on our phone, tablet, computer, etc. But checking it only clutters your head and your inbox. Processing your email involves taking that next step of acting on it.

When you process your email, you make a decision to either DELETE, ACT, FORWARD or FILE it.

DELETE   Do you really need this email? If not, trash it. Ask yourself, "if I go to find this email and it's not there, what's the worst thing that can happen to me?" If you can live with the answer, DELETE IT! Avoid the clutter and let it go.

ACT   NEWS FLASH! Your inbox was designed
               to hold only emails that require ACTION.
               That's it. If there's some kind of action
               associated with an email, then keep it in
               your inbox. Your inbox soon begins to
               turn into a task list.

FORWARD   Yep, this is an action as well but it doesn't
               take much time. Once you determine an
               email should be forwarded, pass it on.
               Then you can delete it and get it out of
               your inbox.

FILE   Most people don't leverage the filing
               capabilities in their email. You can create
               email folders to store all of your emails
               just like you would in a file cabinet.
               Create and organize your email files so
               that at any given time you can find what
               you're looking for easily.

ACTION

In order to lead your email, you have to start to create
new email habits. Read over this list of action items from
Patty to see what you can begin to implement right
now…today!

1. **Unsubscribe**. Every client tells me they get so many
   emails that they never read but they are afraid they'll
   miss something. Unsubscribe from lists that you no
   longer want or enjoy. You're welcome.

2. **Schedule time to check your email.** This is usually a low energy task, so schedule it appropriately. First thing in the morning might not be your best option.

3. **Process your email daily.** Don't let your email pile up. It will become a chore to go through it all at once.

4. **Close your email program when you are not using it.** That way it won't pull you in so easily.

5. **Put aside your personal and non-urgent messages for last.** These can take you away from important work.

6. **Use filters.** Many email programs have a filter that will allow you to route messages from specific recipients or messages containing certain keywords into pre-determined folders.

7. **Mark emails as unread or use follow-up flags** (if available). If an email needs action, mark it as unread or use a follow-up flag (in tools) that will signify that you still need to deal with that email. Try to keep your inbox as empty as possible.

8. **Make friends with your delete button.** Don't be afraid to get rid of something unless you know you will need it later.

9. **Right-click for new subfolders.** Using subfolders to immediately organize incoming email is helpful in keeping your inbox organized and clutter-free.

10.   **When sending email, keep it simple.** Use email to your advantage but consider if a phone call may be easier and be less time consuming than going back and forth with email tag.

BONUS TIP!

In Microsoft Outlook, you can change the subject of an email in your inbox to reflect the action you need to take rather than the subject that the email came with. Just Google "change subject in Outlook (your version year)" to find out how. It varies for each version.

Remember: any time you check your email, make a conscious effort to process it. Don't just read it and jump to the next one. Process it first with DELETE, ACT, FORWARD, or FILE.

Bottom line: Take control of your email. Don't let email control you.

Lead your time

Are you a planner who doesn't plan?

If you're not in control of your time, our guess is that you don't really – and we mean *really* – plan your day. Now let's address the reality of it all: having your plan in your head or a to-do list on your desk is not a plan. Your calendar is the perfect tool to plan and run your day. We'll get to this shortly.

The most ironic phenomena that we've encountered is that financial *planners* plan for everyone but themselves. It's another huge internal barrier that stands between where you are and where you want to be. Too many financial planners don't plan their day, week, month, goals, or intentions. Planning for these responsibilities is as important as planning for your client's future.

Leading your time begins with your ability to protect your time. That's right – protect your time. You are the commander-in-chief of your time and therefore your calendar. You and only you can protect it and thereby influence your productivity. Look at it this way; you have 24 hours in a day, 168 hours in a week, 8760 hours in a year.

- How do you want to spend these hours?

- Do you like the way you are spending them now?

- Are you as productive as you possibly can be during each 24-hour day?

- How much quality time do you give to your children, spouse, partner, family, friends, and other important people and activities in your life?

Somehow, barriers get in the way of your intentions. You know what you want to do with your time, but it never happens that way. If what you want and what you do are not in alignment, then you need to take steps to adjust that. Let's look at six solid strategies to help you balance your time and lead the time-wasters in your life rather than them leading you.

Adjust your reality

Have you ever started out doing a task and then run out of time? You thought you had scheduled plenty of time to complete it, but that didn't work out so well. If you tend to be someone who underestimates the amount of time it takes to do certain tasks, you probably go home at the end of the day feeling like you completed nothing of significance. We hear this a lot, so we have a simple fix. All you need to employ is a timer. Any timer will do; you can use the timer on your phone, computer or even kitchen stove, as long as it's a timer. (Cool tip: if you enter "Google 10 minute timer" in your browser, it will begin to count down from 10 minutes instantly. Just type in the number of minutes you want and it'll start there.)

Determine the amount of time you think a task will take and set the timer for that amount of time. For example, if you have a task you think will take only 15 minutes, set a timer for 15 minutes and work diligently until the timer goes off. If on a regular basis, you are not done with the task at hand, you know your sense of time reality is off and needs an adjustment.

ACTION

Create a document to track how long things actually DO take vs. how long you thought they would take. Track your time for a week to find your new reality. This exercise will give you a good sense of where you are way off compared to reality. Then stop kidding yourself and start scheduling your time more realistically.

Schedule your to-do list

You've been running like crazy all day, never stopping. It feels like you've been so busy, yet you have crossed nothing off of your to-do list. In fact, to make yourself feel better, you add something to your to-do list that you actually accomplished just so you have something to cross off!

When time seems to evaporate before your very eyes, planning becomes the hero of the day. If you already have a to-do list on paper you've taken the first step. Most women advisors we know keep their to-do list in their heads. The problem is, that list is in there with everything else you need to worry about or do before the end of the day. We call this situation the swirls because everything just swirls in your head all day AND all night, waking you out of a deep sleep at 2 am. Has your mental to-do list caused you to wake up in the middle of the night?

Of course, putting your to-do list on paper is good, but it's not enough. In order for your to-do list to be acted on and completed, it requires that time be dedicated to the tasks, and it demands commitment on your part. The best way to dedicate time to your tasks is to use your calendar as a planning tool. The following action will completely change how you plan and view your day.

ACTION

It's time to make *decisions*. Since everything on your to-do list is something you can easily avoid, we need to engage your *decision*-maker to put an end to this avoidance. One by one, take each task on your list and *decide* when you can do it and enter it in that time slot on your calendar. By doing this, you are scheduling an appointment with yourself to complete each task.

We know that this internal barrier to avoid some tasks is quite tall. We also know that sometimes the world turns upside down and you will skip right over that task and move on to the next thing without giving it a second thought. If this happens, *decide* on a new day and time that you can complete it, and renew your commitment to completing that chore.

This barrier might take some time to hurdle, especially if your *decision*-making muscle is weak, so stick with it. Remember, you're leading your time. You must make the commitment and lead yourself to follow through. Persistence and crisp *decision*-making are how you chip away at this barrier.

Motivate your procrastinator

We should have saved this section until the end for the procrastinators reading this (but we didn't.)

Sometimes the barrier to putting things off might be hard to identify. Perhaps you simply procrastinate. You've become really good at avoiding the things you can't stand to do until the pressure is so high that you have no other option but to stay late and get it done.

Procrastination is the art of putting off
until tomorrow what can be done today.

It's a key contributor to poor time management and has caused many people to lose sleep, money, happiness, and probably years from their lives. Procrastination can inflict worry, stress, and fear just from the knowledge that you will have to finish doing things at the last minute.

The big question is **why** do we procrastinate? The answer can be simple: it's easier not to do the task because you don't like to do it. Or it can be more complex. For instance, rather than allowing yourself to feel overwhelmed, you intentionally avoid thinking about the task until the last minute.

We don't claim to be psychologists. However, we do help female advisors just like you every day, some of whom have become expert procrastinators. Let's look at some causes and then explore some simplistic, practical ways for handling your internal barrier of procrastination that we know have worked for other advisors.

Procrastination Barrier #1

It is easier NOT to do something than it is to do it.

Remember how you just read about leading your to-do list? It's one thing to not have a grip on your to-do list, but when you're not getting things done, it could be a symptom of this bigger problem – procrastination.

If you like to make to-do lists (either in your head or on paper), you may look up and down your list and gravitate towards the easier, lower priority tasks. It's easy to scan right over the less-than-attractive, important tasks. Simply put, this is human nature.

Your mind is telling you: "If you complete the easy stuff first or the things you most enjoy, at least you'll be able to cross something off your list." Right?

Crossing something off your list is very gratifying. However, sometimes, the more important things really need your attention. Patty's co-author, the late Steven Covey, author of *The Seven Habits of Highly Effective People*, introduced us to the four quadrants of time management organized by urgency and importance as you'll see on the next page. Perhaps a basic appreciation for these quadrants will help you learn to prioritize your tasks so that you can see the importance of doing some tasks before others.

The Four Quadrants

	Urgent	Not Urgent
Important	Important & Urgent	Important & Not Urgent
Not Important	Not Important & Urgent	Not Important & Not Urgent

If you take a minute to sort your tasks into these four quadrants, it will quickly become obvious which tasks require your more immediate attention, despite whether the job is easy or not. Now carry on with the next action step.

ACTION

Again, schedule *all* of your to-do items in specific time slots in your day planner (make this decision and commitment.) Be sure to pay particular attention to your "important & urgent" tasks as they require your immediate attention. Next, focus on your "important & not urgent" obligations, and then "urgent & not important." By making a commitment to schedule your to-do list based on importance and urgency, you will check off a much higher percentage of tasks at the end of the day.

ONE MORE ACTION …

Are you pushing a task forward day after day? If so, confront it. Ask yourself if there is someone else that could or would do it for you. If it is something that you just aren't good at, maybe you should consider educating yourself in that area so the task seems less daunting. Ask others how they do it since there might be a better or easier way of which you are unaware.

Procrastination Barrier #2

The task or project seems SOOOOOO overwhelming.

Does this scenario sound familiar to you? Let's say you have a huge project ahead of you. You know it's going to take at least 30 hours to accomplish and you have six months to do it. Now that sixth month is here and you are scrambling to get it all done in a very limited amount of time.

This is *not* healthy and can cause major amounts of absolutely preventable stress.

ACTION

Question: How do you eat an elephant?
Answer: One bite at a time

The same concept applies to your project. Don't look at this giant task as a 30-hour impossible project. Instead, remember the elephant. Retrain your brain to think of this project as six 5-hour projects. That means you only have to work on it for five hours per month over the next six months! Isn't that much more tolerable? Some might take it even further by breaking the five-hours per month into five 1-hour projects (one hour per week) and scheduling each one-hour chunk into a time slot in their calendar. Doesn't that project seem much more manageable now?

What project do you have on your plate now that could be broken down into smaller chunks?

Procrastination Barrier #3

You don't know where to start.

Finding a starting point can always be tricky. It's sort of like writer's block. Every author has their personal strategies that work for triggering their words. Some may need to take a walk, others listen to music, and some may listen to an audiobook for inspiration.

Everyone is different so we have some insight that might help when you feel stuck.

ACTION

Similar to the elephant, many financial advisors find it very helpful to break down a project into small pieces. First, determine all the things that need to be done to complete the project. By doing this simple assessment, you will usually discover that the project isn't nearly as overwhelming or difficult as you first thought. Then carefully examine all the small pieces and look for the one thing that seems easy enough to complete and isolate it as a starting point.

Here's an example: Imagine that you really want to organize your whole office but don't know where to start. It's an overwhelming task. You would start by narrowing it down to your desk (still too big), and then a specific drawer (manageable). Narrowing the task will get you started, and you can then move on to the next drawer, then to the top of the desk, and so on in small steps.

You may be saying, "But I work best under pressure. I love to make a deadline and to feel that rush of adrenaline I get when I'm under the gun." This may be true, but it could be that you have never tried to do something ahead of time to compare how you feel without that rush.

You have probably developed a habit of waiting until the last minute without even knowing it. To see if you are ready to break your procrastination habit, try to work on a task by breaking it down into manageable bites and scheduling them far in advance so you can enjoy the freedom from worry. We think you'll like it!

Manage your interruptions

Perhaps you've experienced the office social butterfly standing in your doorway sharing a never-ending story of something seemingly pointless. You feel trapped. Your colleague is obviously not very aware of the signals you're sending out, either. She or he is tone-deaf to body language. While you don't want to hurt your co-worker's feelings, you know you've got a lot of planning work to do and simply don't have time for this interruption. How do you tactfully get this person out of your office, or more importantly, how do you stop this associate from ever coming into your office when you're obviously busy? Read on.

Let's take a closer look at that office social butterfly or, more generally, the multiple sources of interruptions. No matter what, you're going to have interruptions in your day. Many. We get it. This brings us to another universal truth:

> *Stop being surprised by interruptions*
> *because they're going to happen.*

The key is to plan for them, be proactive, and prepare yourself to handle them. Remember it's up to you to protect your time.

It's a tough situation to be in when there's someone standing in your doorway or sitting in a chair in your office and you haven't invited that person in. Some advisors we know purposely don't have an extra chair in their office to avoid having people sit in their space. This ploy might feel extreme but it works!

There are several strategies that can be employed to help you manage this time sucker. (We had another client who actually cut off 3 inches from the 2 front legs of the extra sitting chairs in his office. This was VERY uncomfortable for guests and they didn't stay long at all. Not recommended but effective, nonetheless. But we digress….)

Maintaining the sanctity of your office space begins with setting boundaries with your time. You can set boundaries in various ways. Let's start with your words.

1. Politely tell people who come into your office that you only have "x" minutes to give them because you are focused on a specific project.

2. Tell them it would be better for them to come back at a certain time when you will have more time to give them your full attention.

3. Even better, tell them you can't talk now but you will come to find them once you've completed your task.

All of these strategies help you keep control of your time and manage the plethora of unexpected drop-in interruptions.

Many times, though, you're the person with the answers. You're the person others need to speak with in order to make a decision. You're the one the client wants to speak to *now*. These interruptions should be managed a little differently than the doorway lurker. A woman advisor we know has successfully trained her office staff to know that when her door is closed, she is focused on something specific and prefers not to be interrupted. And when her door is open, she is open for limited interruptions and will entertain questions and other necessities. In order to avoid being labeled an unapproachable hermit, it's important to make yourself available at some point. If you try this closed/open door strategy, you'll probably be surprised by how quickly people will begin to respect your wishes.

Another idea that we've offered to offices with multiple people is the Red Hat Solution. This strategy involves the team agreeing that anyone can wear the red had for a maximum of say 2 hours per week. While that hat is on, that person is invisible. This provides each team member the opportunity to hyper-focus on a task that needs his or her attention without interruptions. It works! If you don't look good in a red hat, you can designate a scarf or some other accessory that won't mess up your hair.

We know how difficult it is to refocus yourself once you've been interrupted, and this lag time can seriously interfere with your productivity. The numbers are staggering. In 2015, *The Washington Post* published an article written by Brigid Schulte that highlighted a study on the impact of interruptions on your productivity.

Researchers at the University of California, Irvine, found after careful observation that the typical office worker is interrupted or switches tasks, on average, every three minutes and five seconds. And it can take 23 minutes and 15 seconds just to get back to where they left off. Jonathan Spira, author of the book, *Overload! How Too Much Information Is Hazardous to Your Organization*, estimates that interruptions and information overload eat up 28 billion wasted hours a year, at a loss of almost $1 trillion to the U.S. economy. Staggering!

The circled area below shows the area of difficulty in recovering from an interruption. The interruption happens, your energy drops from what you were doing as you take care of the interruption. Then trying to regain that energy is where the difficulty lies. If you have a plan in place to refer to, the recovery time is accelerated considerably. Without a plan, it is likely that you will seek another task, find a time-waster (social media, surfing) or go fill your coffee cup.

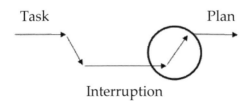

Task   Plan

Interruption

In order to stay focused on the goal to increase your productivity, you must reduce or eliminate your typical electronic interruptions. We call this attention management. Attention management is learning to manage all the things that take your attention away from what you're supposed to be doing. Take a minute to listen to all the bells, whistles, dings, beeps, and rings surrounding you. Every time you hear one of those sounds, you've been trained to respond like Pavlov's dog. Some studies have shown that we get interrupted 3 times every minute. This can seriously impact your productivity if you respond to each one of those distractions! The answer?

ACTION

Turn it off. Yes. Everything. Turn off the ding you hear and the shadow envelope you see every time you get an email. Turn off the IM and Facebook notifications on your phone. Set your office phone to 'do not disturb' during your focus times. On most cell phones, you can set it to 'do not disturb' and include exceptions if needed like mom, kids, or spouse so they still can get through to you if needed. (That is, of course, if they are not your biggest interrupters.)

Limit your choices

Do you find yourself saying 'yes' to too many things? Do you genuinely enjoy the commitments you've said 'yes' to? Especially things that you really don't have time for but no one else volunteered to do yet the task must get done somehow? Ok, raise your hand if you're guilty! Yes, we know. You're not alone; we've heard it many times before from our clients.

Are you saying 'yes' to things that are not in alignment with your needs and values? Saying 'yes' to too many requests leaves little time for the responsibilities that really matter. This is not rocket science. However, as women, we've been programmed by our culture to say 'yes' because we are supposed to be helpful. We can't help it – or can we? The best news is that, yes, you can help it. You are in charge of YOU when you lead yourself. Everything you do or don't do is a choice.

As a female financial advisor, rarely is anyone telling you what to do, when to do it, or where to be. Therefore, you do have choices, a lot of choices. How many women do you know who struggle with saying 'yes' to too many things? Our experience shows that men can also be guilty of this acquiescent behavior as well.

Consider this perspective. Imagine a circle that has been cut into 24 pieces of a pie, each slice representing one hour of a 24-hour day. When you say 'yes' to something, you are saying 'no' to something else. You see, the pie doesn't get any bigger, so something has to give. It can't happen any other way. The minute you say 'yes' to having a client meeting at 7:00 pm, that means that you have just said 'no' to your family time tonight. The minute you say 'yes' to a morning walk, you just said no to your morning prep time in the office. 'Yes', I'll serve on the board; I'll just say 'no' to getting eight hours of sleep each night. We all get only one 24-hour pie each day, and it is up to each of us to choose how we want to eat it.

ACTION

You want to work backwards here. Instead of taking what time is left for what is important, block off the important things first. Put 'sleep' on 8 of those hours (or whatever number of hours of sleep you need each night), then pull out your needs and values and claim the number of hours for each task that will allow you to live in alignment within that 24 hours. Whatever is left is the amount of time you can spare in order to say 'yes' to something else.

Design your 24-hour Pie

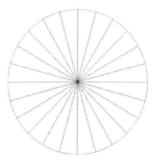

To create another visual, think of a scale in a perfectly equal state. This represents balance in your work and personal life. One day, you accept a new board of director position and the scale starts to tip in one direction. In order to recover your balance, you need to let something go on that same side (stepping down as chair of a committee, not renewing your membership to an organization that no longer improves your life, etc.) Something on that same side must go in order to return to balance.

It's like when you are decluttering and organizing an area of your life. To bring order to your space, we encourage you to enforce the one-in/one-out rule (see Patty's book, *But I Might Need It Someday*.) When something new comes into your life, you must get rid of something old to make room for it. Makes sense, right? If you buy a new pair of shoes, get rid of a pair of your spouse's. (We're never picky about whose shoes they are as long as one comes in and one goes out. Just don't let your spouse read this. At least that's how we productivity experts would like it to work for you.)

Does this one-in/one-out balance always happen? Not usually. Often times, you create a snowball effect by saying YES to several things in a row and before you know it, you find yourself in over your head. This overreach does nothing but add more stress to the equation, and stress equals imbalance.

A perfect example of overextending yourself can often be seen in the month of September. Whether you have children or not, everyone starts buckling down in September after a summer filled with vacations, fun, and an overall more relaxed work routine. As with the beginning of a school year, businesses and associations also begin to pick up speed with their programs and projects. Based on history, you know you are going to have a hectic fourth quarter, yet you still step up and volunteer to do some work at your children's school, for your professional associations, and on special projects at the firm. This is where you can get into a lot of trouble.

These examples of internal barriers are real and rob you of valuable time and productivity. How can you stop the madness and finally gain control of (or lead) your time and calendar?

Patty writes extensively about this in her book, *The Power of Simplicity – Choosing to live your life on purpose.* Perhaps you are very happy with how you manage your time and there is nothing about it that you would change. If so, we say keep on doing what you are doing because it is obviously working for you.

However, if you are not quite there yet, you need to understand that the **choice** to take control of your time and life is yours to make. Nobody else can do it for you. Sure, we can all find a way to blame how we spend our time on someone else. The best thing to do if this describes you is to look in the mirror. If the following statements represent something you would say, this may indicate that you are not in control of your time:

- When my clients need to see me, I schedule a meeting according to their availability.

- I go to my client's home or office because it is more convenient for them.

- When we set any appointments, we never include or announce an end time because I want to be sure we have time to get everything done.

- When anyone in my family needs anything, they always come to me because they know I'll drop everything and take care of them.

- People in my life – at home and work – expect me to do everything because I never say no and never let them down.

Almost 100% of the financial advisors that we coach have complete control over their day. In other words, nobody tells them what to do or where to be at any given time. *It's up to them to choose how they want to plan their day.* That last sentence provides a clear definition of freedom! If you are in complete control of your day but feel like it gets completely out of control quickly and often, then it's time to buckle down and start to plan.

As the guardian of your own time, it's important to think smart and schedule your time with intention. The raw truth is that if you don't control your time, someone else will. It happens every day. Your calendar is a primary tool for managing your time. But before you can learn how to leverage your calendar more productively, we need to introduce you to your Ideal Week.

Your ideal week is designed based on the answer to this question: If you had 100% control of your time when you woke up every Monday morning, what would your Ideal Week look like?

Knowing what your Ideal Week looks and feels like for you becomes something to strive for each week. We are very realistic in knowing that you may never fully attain your 'ideal' week because of outside influences, but the goal is to get a lot closer to that ideal week than you are right now. Having that vision will be the key.

> *Without a vision of your Ideal Week,*
> *how will you know if you've attained it?*

A major component of the Ideal Week is time blocking. This is one of the best strategies to help you gain control of your calendar and make better choices. However, it takes ongoing accountability to change behavior. Evidence supports the fact that time chunking can increase your productivity. Here's what the notion of 'ideal' might look like:

- I only want to see clients on Tuesdays and Thursdays.

- I'll do admin and clients services on Monday mornings.

- I will attend my networking group on Wednesday mornings.

- I will call or meet prospects and COIs on Wednesday afternoons.

- I will leave the office at 1 pm on Fridays.

- I'll do my financial planning work on Monday afternoons and Friday mornings.

ACTION

You can design your Ideal Week however you like but be sure to create it to suit your lifestyle. You can design your Ideal Week by opening an Excel spreadsheet and putting your working hours down the left-hand axis in half-hour increments and adding the days of the week along the top. Then fill in these timeslots as you would like them to look.

	SU	M	T	W	TH	F	SA
6:00							
6:30							
7:00							
7:30							
8:00							
↓							

You'll also want to include things in your Ideal Week that you want to do regularly.

For example:

- I leave work at 5 pm every day.
- I take lunch from 12:00-1:00 pm every day.

- I work out from 6:30-7:00 am.
- I work from home on Mondays.
- I take my kids to school every morning at 8:00 am.
- I go to yoga Tuesday and Wednesday at 6:30 pm.

The easy part is creating the Ideal Week. The true challenge is living it. By creating this Ideal Week, you can plan your days and weeks accordingly. This Excel template becomes your compass for planning!

Say 'no' more often

As we mentioned earlier, managing your time and saying 'yes' to everything actually makes for a conflict of interest. It's really challenging to take control of your time if you can't control two simple words in the English language – 'yes' and 'no.'. This internal barrier can get you into a lot of trouble and steal your time right out from under you. You know exactly what we mean because you, and so many women advisors like you, can't say 'NO.' Well, we believe you can. We know it's possible because we've helped many financial advisors not only gain control of their time but do it in such a manner that is comfortable for them and creates more balance in their lives.

Saying the actual word 'no' is not hard. Say it with us. 'NO.' Again. NO.'

The hard part is when you're looking someone in the eye and telling them 'no.' It's uncomfortable when you're telling a client 'no.' It's difficult when you're telling your senior partner 'no.' We understand. The truth is, sometimes you simply can't say 'no.' However, we're not talking about those times right now. We're talking about all the times when you do have a choice. If you expect to find any sense of balance in your life, you need to practice saying 'NO.' We suggest that you focus on what you're actually saying 'yes' to when you say 'no' to something else. That will put a smile on your face, and it could quite possibly be life-altering for you.

If you take anything from this book that will immediately impact your life and your practice, THIS IS IT. Before you consider taking on *any* new activity, you need to be crystal clear that there is room in your life for this pursuit *without* sacrificing what matters most to you. Too often, the word 'yes' or 'ok' comes out before you realize the consequences. This is a good time to realize that YES, you have choices, and saying NO is one of them.

> *It is a habit to say YES without*
> *even realizing NO was an option.*

Real life balance relies heavily on the power of the 'pause.' Without it, you keep adding more and more time-consuming activities without conscious thought.

Investing just a few minutes or even seconds in a 'pause' BEFORE anything new enters your life can make a monumental difference. This pause allows you to make a conscious decision whether or not you have both physical and emotional room to take on a new request. Women tend to overlook, ignore, or just don't know about this tiny but super-important space of time. Taking a pause allows you to stop long enough to think about what you are doing. This reflective step escapes many women advisors because they run at such a fast pace that slowing down or stopping momentarily is a foreign concept.

ACTION

Do it now. PAUSE. Breathe.

When you take a moment to pause and consider your options you will feel empowered. That tiny investment of time can help you to reap huge rewards! Here are a few secret tips that can help you say 'no' after allowing yourself a pause to consider any decision more clearly and mindfully.

Tip #1 – Pause and take time to research

When someone asks you to do something, say you will look into it, and then do a little homework. Find out exactly how much time it will take you to be involved with this project or task. Look into the amount of time that's necessary outside of the given task. For example, if it's a board position, consider the day, time of day and length of the board meeting as well as what's expected outside of those board meetings. Consider your needs and values. Speak to those who have gone before you about their experience as well as those with whom you would be serving. This will help you see if you will enjoy the people you'll be working with and the actual things you'll be doing. It might end up that you can politely say, "I can't serve at this time because, after careful consideration, I realized that I just don't have the time. I won't make a commitment that I can't fulfill. I'm sure you can understand. I really appreciate you asking me."

Tip #2 – Pause and consider suggesting someone else

Have you ever noticed how the same people seem to always be the ones who are asked to do everything? You're probably one of those people. Certainly, there are many other people who could also serve on this project or position quite well but haven't been considered. Maybe you know of someone who seems perfect for the position or project instead of you. In that case, you can say, "I can't serve on the board at this time, but I might know someone who is willing. I'll ask her and let you know what she says." Or "I was talking with Mary the other day and I think she might be willing to offer her time and expertise."

NOTE: PLEASE don't throw your friends or colleagues under the bus. It's always best to check with them first before offering them as a volunteer.

Tip #3 – Pause and determine your boundaries

When somebody wants you to do something, always remember that you're the one in the driver's seat. They can't make you do anything you don't want to do. If you truly know your limits and are leading your time, you can say, "I'll be willing to help under these conditions." OR "I can only do this for six months and after that, you will need to find someone else." The bottom line is, if all else fails, balance your life by simply saying "No, thank you." We guarantee more opportunities will be waiting just around the corner.

Remember, when someone asks you to do something, you are likely one of several people on the list to be asked. Others have said no before you, which prompted you to get the next call. You, too, can say no and let the requester call the next name.

When it's your turn, the power of the pause is all about making thoughtful, not impulsive, decisions. It's about allowing yourself time to consider your options carefully and consider the impact your decision will make on your 24-hour pie. Who will gain? Who will suffer?

As you master becoming the leader of your time by adjusting your reality, you are learning to:

1. Schedule your to-do list
2. Motivate your procrastinator
3. Manage your interruptions
4. Limit your choices and say no more often.

Over time, you will gain more freedom. Freedom to be. Freedom to live more intentionally, mindfully and purposefully. The choice is always yours to make.

Learning how to lead YOURSELF in your life and work gives you a strong foundation for leading others. As we move on, you'll see that one of the most powerful assets of a financial advisor is social capital. While social capital encompasses all the relationships in a person's life, for this book, we focus specifically on those relationships that can help you grow your practice or firm so that it better fits your vision. Moving into Section Four we'll focus on your business development and more specifically on how you can leverage your relationships in a comfortable manner, one that is in alignment with your way of doing business, *A Woman's Way.*

SECTION 4

Lead Your Relationships

*"The effectiveness of your work will never rise above
your ability to lead and influence others."*
- *John Maxwell*

Now that we have addressed a multitude of ways for you to lead your productivity in your life and work, it's time to look deeply into how you can lead your relationships for greater results. Becoming the leader of your relationships means being able to influence and leverage your entire network to help grow your practice or firm. It also means accepting the responsibility to act as the leader in all of your relationships, including family, friends, clients, centers of influence (COIs) and your entire network of people. Your role as a leader shows up everywhere and with every relationship: clients, referral sources, networking colleagues, prospects, and even internal colleagues. If you pay attention, where two or more people are interacting, there is always a leader and a follower(s).

John Maxwell, one of our favorite thought leaders on the topic of leadership, says that "leaders tend to initiate and followers tend to react." In his book, *Developing the Leader Within You*, he says:

> Leaders tend to lead, pick up the phone and make contact, spend time planning, anticipate problems, invest time with people, and fill their calendar with priorities. Followers tend to listen, wait for the phone to ring, spend time living day-to-day, react to problems, spend time with people, and fill their calendar with requests.

Read that last quote once again to internalize it. Leaders know what they want and how to get other people engaged in their purpose. Leaders know how to motivate others and keep themselves top of mind. Are you currently a leader or a follower? Maybe you lead some relationships but others not so much.

We know from experience that THE key to success in growing your practice or firm in *A Woman's Way* rests specifically on your ability and willingness to lead your relationships. Leading your relationships is the most significant component of a successful, organic growth strategy. This leadership is not hard, but it does take focus and effort. It involves capitalizing on opportunities to embrace the leadership role when developing reciprocal business relationships. In helping you become leaders in your relationships, we might stretch you a bit here and there, but we will tap into your natural strengths and help you gain more comfort along the way.

Up until now, you may have been feeling that something wasn't quite right with how you are going about business development and getting referrals. The way you've been taught, predominantly a man's way, doesn't quite fit you and often feels uncomfortable. Over the years, you may have heard, "You have to do it 'this way,'" so many times that you've come to believe it's the only way. However, there is never just one way or the only way. Your life and your business are about YOUR way. *A Woman's Way*.

This section is designed to help you lead and leverage your relationships to receive more referrals and grow your practice your way. We're going to benefit from your natural ability to listen, empathize, collaborate, connect with people, develop and nurture relationships, communicate clearly, be creative and compassionate, and understand people with heart. Then, we're going to wrap up all of these natural abilities in a ribbon of structure.

Very often, women advisors find themselves repeatedly giving opportunities and referrals to others while receiving nothing or little in return. We also see women advisors attempting to develop referral relationships with male COIs only to have those COIs pass their referrals to their male advisor counterparts.

Many women struggle to receive referrals. They generally have the leadership qualities necessary for successful referability; however, more often than not, women bury their leader behind a smile. Through our coaching and everyday conversations, we have realized that often women advisors are completely unaware of how their internal barriers erect roadblocks that sabotage or prevent the reciprocity from ever reaching them.

If you're ready to take your referral process into your own hands and lead it to produce what you know is available to you, then keep reading. We are here to walk you through not only what it means to lead your relationships but how to do it successfully and comfortably to grow your practice your way – *A Woman's Way.*

Lead by example

As mentioned earlier, in any relationship (parent/child, partners, business owners, centers of influence, clients, prospects, etc.), there always tends to be a leader and a follower. No doubt that role can switch back and forth depending on the situation. When leaders lead, others tend to follow. That's the concept we want you to embrace when working with your relationships to grow your practice. There's one thing to always remember: *you and only you control the results you get or don't get from your relationships.* For this reason, we ask you to accept the role of leader.

Recognize that by reading this book you already have more information about leading a relationship than perhaps most people you know. With this knowledge comes responsibility. And with responsibility comes leadership.

Let's begin with *leading by example*. For many women, it's hard to ask others for anything. Yep, you guessed it, it's another internal barrier that shows up over and over. We understand. However, to grow your practice, getting past this barrier is very important. Leading by example enables you to do what you do best – help others. But we're not letting you fully off the hook from asking others for something. In this case, you will give others a chance to see how they can help you by helping them first. You will lead the way. This increases your comfort level when it's your turn to ask.

How does leading by example show up in your day? What does this behavior really look like when you connect it to business development and referrals? Simply put, if you want a certain behavior or opportunity to come from someone else, one of the best things to do is to model that behavior or offer that opportunity to others first. Let's consider how leading by example shows up when you're networking.

Kathy came to us with a disdain towards networking. She said that networking made her skin crawl. Admittedly, she would be the first to leave an event because she just couldn't take it any longer. More than anything, she grew frustrated with the conversations that in her words were typically 'more small talk and about useless things like sports and TV shows.'

In Michelle's book, *The 29% Solution*, she discusses how asking your own questions can actually lead a conversation. We applied this strategy when we helped Kathy to see that as a leader of her network, she could influence her networking conversations by asking the type of questions she wanted to discuss. The key was, she had to ask them first. For example, if she wanted to discuss the kinds of clients she works with, she couldn't just stand by and wait for someone to ask her because it probably wouldn't happen. She needed to ask the question, "Can you tell me about the kinds of clients you work with?" first. This would almost always lead to the other person flipping the same question back to Kathy, enabling her to talk about what she wanted to all along. This new practice changed everything for Kathy. In no time, she became the last one to leave an event because now the conversations were interesting and meaningful. She now knew how to lead by example and model what she wanted to have happen. As a leader, others naturally followed her in those conversations.

Leading by example by being the first to step up also helps when you're trying to leverage your relationships. Let's say that you know one of your network colleagues belongs to a professional mom's group. You would really like to attend one of their events as a guest, but you don't want to ask her directly because it feels as though you're imposing. So instead, you invite her to attend an event **with you first**. (Yep, you'll find this strategy in *The 29% Solution*, too). This act of giving can plant a seed in your colleague's head and could naturally lead her to invite you to the mom's group's next event. Or, perhaps having just had a great time together, it's easier for you to now say, "We should do this more often. If there's ever an event that you're going to, I would love to be your guest too."

Allowing someone to help you is a gift, not a curse. Try to remember what it feels like when someone asks you for something. It's powerful to give, and it can be just as powerful to receive because you're letting someone give of themselves and experience that same feeling of joy and fulfillment. We've witnessed that people who only give or only receive are rarely happy or balanced. Because you're leading by example, you're helping the other person to see how they too can leverage their relationships, and so the chain of giving continues.

Here's another scenario of leading by example and being first. Let's assume you know that the estate attorney you refer to has a great blog that gets lots of attention. You would really like to post a blog on her site and get that exposure. Be first. Lead by example. Model what you want to have happen. Ask her if she would write an article for your next newsletter. Tell her you would like to expose her to your clients. This invitation will bring a lot of extra value to the relationship because, in most cases, the human law of reciprocity kicks in and the attorney looks for ways to reciprocate. She might even say, "This is a fantastic idea! What can I do for you?" That's your opportunity to suggest the blog post.

By role modeling this type of giving behavior, you are, in essence, leading your relationships to do more for each other. It's true that some people won't reciprocate and you might have to ask. But more often than not, people do reciprocate. They just didn't think of it first because they are in the follower role of their relationships.

We help to build this type of behavior all the time with our clients. Here are a few more examples.

- If you're looking for a CPA to treat your clients with exceptional service, model that same behavior in return by treating her or his clients exceptionally.

- If you prefer that your referrals from COIs are already expecting your call, model that style of referring to others by delivering referrals that are expecting a call from your COI.

- If you prefer to meet your prospects for the first time in person, model that activity by asking the person you're referring to if they prefer in-person first meetings as well and follow through.

- If you want people to call you back within 24 hours, model that behavior yourself first.

You get the picture. You might be saying, "Oh, this seems so natural," and it might be for you, but it's not natural for everyone. Remember, we're tapping into your natural strengths and what you are good at may not be easy or natural for others.

We find that so many people get mired in their daily grind and tasks that many of these little cues get missed, yet these little prompts really do matter. They actually matter so much that people will often remark on how refreshing you are to work with, and before you know it, you will be influencing the behavior of others. We've seen it happen over and over.

One of our female advisor clients, Sara, is a good example. Sara has a great relationship with Jill, a CPA. Sara knows that Jill often has her clients in her office when she discovers that they really need Sara's help. She knows that Jill will say to her client, "You really should consider calling Sara for help with this. Here's her card." However, we all know what happens in that case, right? Usually, nothing.

Typically, Sara would never hear from the prospect. What Sara really wanted was for Jill to pick up the phone on the spot and schedule a meeting with all three of them at Jill's office. Sara knew that simple act would make all the difference because once the prospect met her with Jill's endorsement, she was almost guaranteed a new client. So, Sara began leading by example. When she had a referral for Jill, she would pick up the phone, call Jill, and schedule a meeting with all three.

In no time at all, Jill quickly picked up on how awesome it was to have someone do that on her behalf, and she started reciprocating the behavior back to Sara. This change in behavior occurred because Sara accepted the leadership role in her relationship with Jill, and she demonstrated that leadership in her actions. Jill was willing to reciprocate, and the referral relationship took a huge step forward.

Leading by example really works. One thing to remember as a leader is that you always need to be a step ahead and a little creative. For example, you need to:

- Know what questions you want to ask when networking

- Know where your people are networking if you want to join them

- See opportunities for you to get greater exposure

- Take an inventory of what you have to offer to those in your network that could trigger reciprocity for you in some way.

Don't get confused, however. **This is NOT about taking advantage.** Taking advantage is a one-way gain. This is about leadership. When you lead, everyone gains!

Before switching gears, we want to point out the key role Jill played in our last example. Jill is a perfect COI for Sara, and not just because of the letters CPA behind her name. There's a lot more to their relationship than that. Playing with the right people on your team (your COI team) makes all the difference. Just ask Mike Tomlin, current Head Coach for the Pittsburgh Steelers. (Can't blame us for getting in a hometown plug!) He truly knows the value of having the right players on your team.

Remember, when it comes to leading by example, be first at everything – first to ask questions, first to refer, first to give, first to invite, first to applaud, first to call, first to respond, etc. Before we move on and look at how your leadership skills come into play with picking the right COI relationships, take a moment to act on what you've just read.

ACTION

- Where can you lead by example?
- How would you like to leverage your network?
- What can you offer to your network that brings additional value to others?

For example, do you have a newsletter, a blog, belong to a unique group, have a membership in a club, have an event coming up that someone can attend with you, have a boat that can be used for a prospect outing? You name it!

Make a list now of the added value you can bring to your COIs. If you need additional ideas, check out *The 29% Solution*, Week 15: "Be A Value-Added Friend."

Lead Your COIs

Have you ever had a relationship with a center of influence (COI) that went sour? We hear a lot of frustrated financial advisors complain about COIs. Many advisors we work with describe their experiences with

COI relationships as very one-sided. What we hear is that the advisor tends to give more business than she receives.

One familiar problem often surfaces here: many women advisors seem to go along to get along, and by doing so they end up settling for less. In the long run, in most cases the advisor never says anything to her COIs and instead continues to push forward in frustration. Women don't want to cause friction or engage in conflict if they can help it. So instead they remain quiet. This is an internal barrier that leads plenty of women advisors to spend too much time with the wrong people.

Men, on the other hand, are not too timid to tell others what they want. Women rarely share their expectations with others. Men expect that COIs will refer them, and if they don't get it, they move on to another relationship. Women *hope* their COIs will refer them and typically avoid the conversation when they don't get referrals. We believe it's time for women advisors to raise the bar for themselves, along with their expectations. As you continue reading we'll help you gain the confidence needed to have the kind of relationships you deserve with your COIs.

One example of a woman who was able to raise the bar is our client, Mary, and this is what she discovered. Mary felt the pain of a one-sided COI relationship for several years with a banker. During one of our coaching calls, she was asked to pay attention to how much new business she was passing along to this business banker in her town. During the course of our call, Mary also had the revelation that she had never received any new business in return from the banker. We coached Mary on what to say to the banker and how to have that difficult conversation. Mary was about to raise the bar.

Through Mary's conversation with the banker, she discovered that she was NEVER going to get any business in return because the bank had a policy that was not in favor of referring to outside financial advisors. Despite Mary's excellent reputation in the community, the bank was fearful to refer to an independent advisor and preferred to give their referral business to an advisor connected to a large wirehouse. Mary might never have known the reality of her relationship with this COI until she had "the conversation."

Imagine how much time and aggravation Mary could have saved if she had known this bank policy before entering into this relationship. She may have chosen a different relationship or at the very least been more knowledgeable going in. But like so many other female advisors, Mary never established any expectations with her COI.

If something like this has happened or is happening to you, maybe the communication between you and the COI has simply fallen apart or never really existed from the beginning. This can change, however. You can raise the bar and begin to establish expectations moving forward. And the transition doesn't need to be uncomfortable.

Relationships with COIs can become complex. Nobody said relationships were easy. With COIs, many other issues can come up as well. For example, perhaps the COI performs what you feel to be less-than-stellar work for your client. Or this professional never follows up with a referral you've given. How do you handle these awkward situations? The best answer, of course, is open communication. We help to guide many of these conversations daily.

Consider this analogy. Imagine you are trying to play a song on the piano with your fellow COI and you're playing from page 2 but your COI friend is playing from page 6. Yikes! The two of you might shatter glasses somewhere if you don't drive each other crazy first. This kind of miscommunication is exactly what happens when you fail to enter a relationship on the same page with a COI.

Without open communication and clear expectations supporting the relationship, you could easily end up making false assumptions, operating in the dark, and having completely different expectations from the relationship. We all know what happens when you make faulty assumptions, operate in the dark, or have differing expectations. It's never good!

So how do you find the right people, establish reliable expectations, and create the pattern of behavior that will ultimately improve your referral results? And how do you perform the leadership role and guide the process for a more successful relationship?

1. Know WHAT you're looking for! (Notice we did not say WHO.)

- Do the players on your COI team have what you want?

- Are they genuinely excited about helping you succeed?

- Are they committed to you and willing to reciprocate?

- Are they the kind of people you feel comfortable sending your best client to?

We can pretty much guarantee that some of the COIs you're working with right now are not the right ones for you. In one way (or perhaps more) they are not in alignment with you and/or who you are and how you do business. But it might be impossible for you to know this yet because you have no benchmarks for comparison. Your gut is telling you that there's not a match. Wouldn't it have been nice if you could have avoided this awkward relationship from the beginning?

Imagine if you took some time to think about WHAT you're looking for first. We're talking about the kind of personal qualities that you need to see in your COIs. After all, there's a strong chance that they may be working with your best clients in due time. Don't you want the best? Don't you want them to be in alignment with you? Right now, we see advisors simply putting a vacancy sign outside and accepting through the door just about any COI with the right title (CPA, Estate Attorney, Business Banker, Insurance Broker, etc.). It's no wonder a lot of time and energy are wasted on the wrong people. It's no wonder there is such a high level of frustration with COIs.

What are YOU looking for?

What criteria would you like your COIs to meet in order to pass through your door?

What personal characteristics do you need from your COIs to work together smoothly?

These are two big questions that most advisors never formally consider before entering into a COI relationship. We recommend that this conversation happens at the firm level as well by developing a comprehensive list of qualities and characteristics that are foundationally the minimum for the types of people your firm will deal with as COIs. From there, each advisor like yourself should personalize her list to meet her own requirements.

Here are some examples of personal qualities and characteristics that some of our clients have considered for their requirements:

- ☐ Friendly
- ☐ Fun
- ☐ Great networker

☐ Knowledgeable

☐ Professional

☐ Accessible

☐ Responsive

☐ Ethical

☐ Operates with integrity

☐ Informative

☐ Deeply respected

☐ Volunteers in our community

☐ High client satisfaction

☐ Family-focused

☐ Faith-centered

☐ Relationship builder

☐ Female

☐ Certified/Qualified in their expertise

☐ Minimum 5 Years in Business

What are the qualities and characteristics that are important to you?

As a woman financial advisor, our guess is that your list would be quite different from your male counterparts. Don't be shy and above all, don't settle. Raise the bar. Be specific and in alignment with who you are. This is your opportunity to begin shaping or reshaping your practice from the ground up. Knowing which qualities you are looking for in the people you will refer business to and perhaps, at some point, entrust your clients to, is indeed, critical work.

ACTION

Take some time now while these ideas are hot in your mind and begin creating your own personal list of COI qualities and characteristics. We'll discuss what you'll do with this list a little later.

2. Know what you EXPECT from your COIs and share it.

One of the biggest problems we see with COIs is that expectations were never set forth from the beginning of the relationship. And even if they were, we rarely see any follow-up or checking-in with each other to see how both sides are feeling about the relationship. This oversight often results in frustration and in some cases, the relationship simply fizzles out without any genuine discussion.

There's no question that setting up a COI relationship with clear expectations is a rare happening. You can almost guarantee that this kind of candid communication is not something your COI will be familiar with, so it's going to make you stand out (in a positive way). Many of our clients have heard their COIs say, "Wow, I don't know anyone else who takes their referral process so seriously."

Already knowing what happens when expectations are not articulated should be incentive enough to encourage you to try a new approach with your COIs. There are two BIG caveats with expectations to keep in mind, however.

One is that they are two-sided. If you expect something from your COI, you must be prepared to offer back something you are willing to do on their behalf as well. If not, don't include a discussion of expectations. And two, your list of expectations begins a conversation and is open to modification from your COIs. Their input and the ensuing dialog will form an informal agreement of how the two of you will operate throughout this relationship. This open discussion will also form a foundation which can be reassessed at mid-year to see how the relationship is working for both parties.

Here's a small list of some expectations that many of our clients incorporate into their best practices. Some have created a one-page document to share with COIs, while others use their list as a guide while discussing the relationship with COI partners. The bottom line is to get both parties playing from the same sheet of music.

Sample COI expectations:

- [ ] Let me know once you have spoken with my referral and if/when you plan to meet or connect
- [ ] Return my calls with 24 hours
- [ ] Follow-up on my referrals within 24 hours
- [ ] Let me know if you close the business
- [ ] Meet with me in person to discuss referral opportunities once a month
- [ ] Be willing to refer me to your best client

☐ Refer me consistently throughout the year to qualified prospects

☐ Offer my services in your proposals

☐ Refer me and my company first

☐ Attend one of our annual client events

☐ Provide us with two relevant articles for our client newsletter

☐ Never give out my business card unless the other person agrees for me to call them.

Please realize that we're not asking you to create a COI contract. Instead, we'd like to see you capture all the things you want on paper and share them with your COIs. The ultimate goal is to eliminate frustrations by avoiding ungrounded assumptions, establishing clarity, and building more harmonious relationships from the beginning.

ACTION

Ready, set, go! Now it's your turn. Create your list of COI expectations. Feel free to steal any of the ones listed above if they resonate with you to get you started.

Now that you have a list of COI qualities and characteristics and a list of COI expectations, what should you do with them? It's not going to do you any good to fold up those lists and hide them in a drawer. It's important to use this information.

You have current COIs who need to know you are now taking your referral dynamic to the next level. You will also be meeting new COIs at some point who need to know this information up front before you start working together. Let's look at each situation, starting with your current COIs, regardless of how many referrals they have sent you in the past. Remember this exercise is all about helping you spend your precious time with more of the right people.

Set Expectations with Current COIs

Leaders know what they want. You've done the work to raise the bar, and now you know exactly what characteristics you need in your COIs and what you expect from your COIs. It's time to lead your relationships and get your referral partnerships on the same sheet of music.

First, take your list of qualities and characteristics and hold it against the people you currently consider to be your COIs. Ask yourself these important questions for each person on your list:

- Does this person meet all of the characteristics on my list? If so, great! They're the kind of person you can work best with.
- If not, which qualities are they missing?
- Are you willing to overlook those missing qualities or not?

- If so, you have a new level of understanding about this person and your COI relationship. You can choose to work with this person and take a leadership role to see if the qualities you seek can be uncovered.

For example, if a COI colleague is not a good networker (and that's one criterion on your list), is this something that you can overlook or not? Is this a deal breaker for you? Can you comfortably refer business to a person and gain the reciprocity you seek without this networking characteristic?

If it's a deal-breaker and you're not willing to overlook the missing characteristic, give yourself a few options to consider. You can remain friends and accept that as a COI, this person may not have a big network which may limit opportunities to refer you. OR you can remain friends and stop thinking of this person as a COI.

Either way, you have to be comfortable with your decision because it means that you can now reallocate the referral time you might have invested with this person towards someone who does have all the characteristics you need. It's your choice, and now you can make an informed choice. Remember it's all about having the right people on your team (your referral team that is).

Once you've done some soul searching with your COIs, it's time to act and share your expectations. We believe that current COIs need to know you're stepping up your referral game. They need to know you're serious about referrals. More importantly than that, they need to know you're now being particular about who you spend your time with and to whom you give your referrals. You'll quickly stand out, and they'll quickly notice.

We also understand and know that some women advisors struggle with expressing their expectations and are not fans of confrontation so let's reframe this scenario for a second. A conversation with a current COI about your expectations does not need to be perceived as a confrontation. The objective is a win-win relationship and you're leading this process. AND remember that whatever you expect FROM the other person, you're more than willing to offer in return. This means they stand to benefit just as much as you do. And finally, you're going to give your COIs the opportunity to add their insight and thoughts to the conversation as well, and they are free to opt out if they can't or are unwilling to meet you in the middle. We're simply applying that little ribbon of structure we spoke of earlier to your referral process.

Here's an example of how you might approach a current COI to have this conversation. "Hi Jennifer. I was wondering if you would be open to meeting with me for lunch, my treat. I'm raising the bar with certain elements of my practice this year and I'd love to share them with you."

During the lunch meeting, you might say, "I've been working on how we can enhance our referral relationship. I'm also working to send consistent messages to my COIs so that we are both clear on what we need from each other. I want to show you what I've come up with so far as a list of things I'm willing to do on your behalf, and I hope that you will be able to do the same for me. I'm really open to your input as well so that we can help each other get more business in the year ahead."

Remember that point we made about always being first? If you notice, in the dialogue above you specifically make it all about the other person first. We encourage you to initially focus the attention toward what you intend to do FOR the other person. This should motivate your referral partner and at the very least encourage dialogue around the referral process, and that's one of your main objectives.

Keep in mind that the goal here is to have an open discussion about what you expect from your centers of influence and what they can expect from you in return. Most likely your COIs have never given expectations this much thought before, so you might need to schedule another meeting to have them bring their thoughts and suggestions to you. In the end, you both will have a much deeper understanding of your referral relationship's expectations, and this gives you a solid foundation to return to when you want to evaluate the relationship. We recommend that you evaluate each COI relationship minimally once a year.

ACTION

Ready to practice? Start by looking over your COI list and comparing which characteristics each individual brings to your relationship. Choose your favorite COI as the first one you share your expectations with and get that person on your calendar for a lunch meeting. Working with your favorite person first will allow you to iron out a few kinks and gain some comfort and confidence with this new process.

Set Expectations with New COIs

When you meet someone new who you suspect might be a good COI, keep your list of qualities and characteristics handy and compare her or his behaviors and ways of work to your list. This is the perfect opportunity to use your new tools with fresh COIs. Remember these tools are meant to help you spend time with the right people and build a win-win relationship from the start. When you feel confident that you see someone you can work with, great; begin to build the relationship. If not, keep looking. This is how *A Woman's Way* practice becomes perfectly aligned with who you are. You're not settling any longer for just a COI. You want the right person for YOU.

Once your new relationship is solid enough to begin talking about referrals, it's time to introduce your expectations. Here's an example of how you might introduce this topic to your new potential COI.

"Diane, I'm really excited about working with you to share referrals. I have learned over the years that when my COI relationships start off with a clear understanding of what we expect from each other, the relationship runs more smoothly and we have greater success. The next time we meet for lunch, I'd like to show you my list of activities I'm willing to do on your behalf as a COI, and I hope you will be able to do the same for me. I'm really open to your input as well because I want this to be a win-win relationship for us."

As you can see, the approach is very similar to what you might say to an established COI. The main difference is timing. Initiating a referral relationship with this kind of simple structure helps to ensure deeper understanding, promotes open communication, establishes expectations, and raises the bar overall. Naturally, you can't help but have better relationships as a result. Oh, right, and a more productive referral process will ultimately result in more referrals for both of you.

ACTION

Do you have a new relationship that you're thinking might turn into a good COI? If so, now's the time to introduce this new process into your practice. Follow these steps and work to get that person on your calendar within the next few weeks. It's no good just reading the book if you're not going to implement its practices.

If this referral discussion still feels daunting, consider how happy you are with the way things are right now with your COIs. Typically, when you're not happy with your relationships, there's something out of alignment. Authenticity is a large component of *A Woman's Way* practice. Be true and authentic to yourself by aligning with the right people so they reflect who you are and how you do business. Anything less than this is unfair to you and sure to have you feeling unsettled.

Lead with Education

When it comes to leading your relationships to refer you more business, no one can do it better than you.

If you remember, our football coach Mike Tomlin of the Pittsburgh Steelers believes it's important to have the right players on the team. (Yep, we did it again!) No doubt with the help of the previous segments you're building a great COI team that's aligned with who you are and what you want. But you have other referral sources beyond COIs on your team that you can't ignore. We're talking about your clients, family, friends, neighbors, soccer parents, classmates, past co-workers – you get the picture. Let's not forget the potential role they all play in helping to grow your practice as we move forward.

A good team wins because it has great plays that work well with the specific team members. Good teams use the right plays at the right time. Now that we've leveraged your strength in building relationships to surround yourself with the right COI players, it's time to create some plays to use with the various referral sources mentioned above. In our world of helping advisors get more business, our great plays come in the form of great supporting tools, productive strategies, well-thought-out plans and proven techniques. Let's get started building your personal business development playbook *A Woman's Way.*

A lot of advisors we work with never make the time (or take any time, for that matter) to **teach** people how to refer them effectively. Think about it. It's one thing for people to know WHAT you do. It's an entirely different thing for people to know HOW to refer you.

Let's consider your current client list. We can almost guarantee that you have clients out there who would refer you in a heartbeat! Right? Some of them have probably even told you they would refer you. But if you're being honest with yourself, the reality is that few of them actually follow-up and do it. Why?

It's not because they don't like you. It's actually quite the contrary. You're great at building those relationships, and they love you like family. Our clients tell us stories all the time about how their clients give them hugs every time they see them and hand deliver cookies "just because."

It's not because they don't know what you do, either. After all, they are your client so they experience your services first hand.

The reason your clients don't typically refer you is that they *don't recognize an opportunity for you* and even if they do, they're not quite sure how to talk about you. Julie Littlechild, the owner of Absolute Engagement, recently confirmed what we've always known and addressed this inability to recognize referral opportunities in her recent research on the topic of why clients don't refer. On her blog posted April 4, 2018, she said, "According to our latest research with high net worth investors, 64 percent of clients who didn't refer in the last year said it was because they simply hadn't met anyone they thought needed a financial advisor. A further 18 percent said it was because they didn't know who to refer." Most advisors believe that clients don't refer because they don't like to talk about money. In fact, Julie showed that actually that discretion only accounts for about 19% of clients.

If clients don't know how to recognize a referral for you, the natural result is nothing will happen. And you sit there waiting for something to happen. Remember, that's a behavior of a follower, not a leader. In this case, such passivity becomes a HUGE internal barrier.

A similar scenario happens with your COIs. You know, beyond a shadow of a doubt, that some of your COIs are in front of prospects for you all day long. If that's the case, why aren't they referring you? Why aren't they thinking of you? The same questions apply to your family, friends, classmates, etc. Of course, the answer to why they're not thinking of you is mostly because they're all wrapped up in their own complex days.

Simply put, you're not top of mind. They don't see the opportunity. You're not a priority for them, and you haven't made it easy for them to refer you. Wow, that's quite a hit in the gut, right? Sometimes the truth is painful. No doubt with your leadership skills honed and your focus in the right place, we can change this scenario.

If you've done the work to establish expectations with COIs and have good players, then all you need to do is teach them how to refer you effectively. Eliminate the belief that your COIs and clients should already know how to refer you because if they did, we wouldn't be writing this section or having this conversation. Eliminate the belief that people don't talk about money – they do.

Now is the time when you have the opportunity to influence your own referral process by becoming a proactive leader. And real leadership takes guts! And it takes trust in your relationships, too. One of the greatest strengths of most women is their ability to build solid, long-lasting relationships. Typically, women advisors nurture their relationships far deeper than men and take great pride in the closeness and high level of trust they create with their clients. Unfortunately, too often that level of trust only goes one way. If you truly trusted your relationships, you would believe and trust that your clients, COIs, friends, and so on *really do* want to help you. However, they need your guidance to make it happen. Instead, we see women advisors worry that if they ask for referrals or help with introductions, their clients will leave them, see them as needy or desperate, or perhaps not like them any longer.

We are asking for you to trust and believe that your clients, COIs, and friends really do want to help you. This new orientation might also take some courage because we know that many (and we mean many) women advisors simply don't want or like to ask for help or for referrals. Let's not get confused, though. Right now, we're focusing on **teaching other people how to refer you**, not so much on how to directly ask for referrals. That part will come later.

Before you can engage your network and teach others how to refer you, you first must get a clear and concise sense of who you are and what you bring to the professional table so that you can articulate it to others well. People can't read your mind. The clearer you are with what you want, the more likely you are to be successfully referred.

Let's start by tapping into your natural educator. Stop and think for a moment about how many people you have taught to do something successfully. If you have kids, that list would include them too. If you don't have kids, think of nieces and nephews, co-workers, parents, grandparents, friends, etc. and all the things you've helped them learn. Your list is likely impressive and surely you're missing some people that you forgotten about teaching.

For the purpose of helping people learn how to refer you well, we've got to start at the beginning by asking yourself the question, "Who do you do your best work for?" Who do you want as clients? In marketing terms, who is your target market? One of our clients, Cindy, recently sent a marketing survey to her firm's COIs (several of whom were also her clients) in order to assess why she was not getting as many referrals as she thought she should. Cindy was surprised to discover that her COIs were confused. The results actually showed that Cindy's COIs did not know who her target market was and so it became unclear who the firm really wanted as clients.

CONFUSION is the kiss of death for your referral process!

When people don't know who to refer to you, they simply won't refer out of fear of not getting it right. No one wants to look bad. Cindy's survey provides a great example of why clarity in who you want as clients is so important.

While this information is making your wheels turn we'd like to share an observation we've been noticing about financial advisors and their target markets. We've begun to notice a trend in the financial profession with more and more firms and financial advisors fine-tuning their services to a niche market. The benefits of serving a niche are quite broad. From a marketing perspective, a niche market is a true specialty area and allows you to:

- Articulate your services in a manner that relates specifically to your market

- Connect with your prospects on a deeper level

- Fine tune all of your marketing efforts

- Build focused COI relationships

- Network more strategically

- Save money through strategic marketing efforts

- More easily become known as the expert in that niche

- Separate yourself from your competition

- Create a truly unique selling proposition

- Significantly increase the return on your marketing investment.

The nature of a niche market also provides the opportunity for your name and services to be passed frequently from one person to another as your prospects all run in the same circles. Serving a niche market is also a great way to separate yourself from your competition. A niche market is highly referable because once people know your niche, you stay top of mind more easily.

For example, for us, since we serve only financial advisors (with a special interest towards female financial advisors) and our network clearly knows our niche, the minute they hear "financial advisor" or "wealth management" they think of us and no one else. Our website – www.ProductivityUncorked.com - clearly reaches out to our niche in words and images that resonate with financial advisors. Our niche drives everything we do.

To give you an example of the kinds of target markets that other wealth management firms are serving right now, we looked at the 2014 *FPA Research & Practice*

Institute Report called "Drivers of Business Growth Study." The most successful firms were following this practice of serving a specific niche. Here are a few:

- Airline pilots
- Physicians
- Executive women
- Divorced women
- Divorced men
- Firefighters
- Law enforcement
- Journalists
- Healthcare professionals
- Teachers
- Veterans
- Widows
- Widowers
- Engineers
- College professors
- Municipal employees
- Non-profits
- LGBTQ community
- Business owners
- Attorneys

Is this focus on niche markets resonating with you? Do you do your best work for a specific group of people because of some unique connection you have with that group? This has proven to be the case for our client, Nina.

Nina is a millennial. She has friends who are millennials. She hangs out with lots of millennials, especially ones that have money and even more so, have great money-earning potential. It's easy for her to relate to them because she is a millennial herself. She understands their needs, their wants, their dreams, and their struggles. As we worked together, she realized how challenging it would be for her to be referred by a 62-year-old CPA. Why not focus her energies where she already has credibility, connects easily, and enjoys the company? After refocusing her marketing message and her efforts, she landed a 1.5-million-dollar client and you guessed it, he was a millennial.

Now it's time for you to take action and begin to capture the essence of what clients you want to do business with all day, every day.

ACTION

Grab a piece of paper and write down the following:

- Who do you want to work with as your client?
- Who do you do your best work for?

Create a profile of your perfect client by answering these questions.

- [ ] What do you know about them?
- [ ] Where do they hang out?
- [ ] What do they value?

- ☐ What are they motivated by?
- ☐ What personal qualities and characteristics do they possess?
- ☐ Why do you like working with them?
- ☐ What is it about them that makes you want to duplicate them?
- ☐ How do you connect with them?

If it makes it easier, imagine putting 3-5 of your favorite clients into a bucket and punching a bunch of holes in the bottom of the bucket. What comes out of the holes are all the things these clients have in common.

These exercises are designed to help you capture the essence of your perfect client. Keep in mind that this is **your** *perfect* **client**, not necessarily your *only* client (unless you truly specialize). If you have or want a niche market, allow yourself to get specific and detailed with your description. Always remember, you will receive what you ask for. Like our client Cindy, since her firms' COIs were confused, their referrals reflected a big variety of prospects, many of which were not a good fit for the firm. However, when Nina specified millennials as her niche market and got very detailed in her description, she was referred to a millennial.

But wait, there's more! What else do you need to teach people in order to get more referrals?

Put yourself in your client's or COI's shoes. You've just taught them who you want as clients. What's next? How will they know if someone is a good prospect for you?

Yes, they need more. They need to be able to recognize an opportunity for you. Remember this inability to recognize a good prospect for you is the number one reason why clients don't refer you. However, you already know how to identify a referral opportunity for yourself because it's all in your head. Now, you have to capture that information and be able to share it with others.

The next question to ask yourself is, "What, specifically, can my COIs and clients see or hear that would trigger them to know that someone might be a good prospect for me?" In other words, how might someone recognize your perfect prospect by simply paying attention? Most of our clients find zeroing in on a perfect client to be a bit of a challenge because they don't necessarily think of their practice this way.

To get you started with this new perspective, we'll share a few thoughts from our client Ellen who, in the most general terms, wants her perfect client to be the "millionaire next door." Her favorite clients make good money, but they don't flaunt it too much. Some things that she wants her COIs and clients to notice might be if someone has a small business, owns rental property, has a get-a-way cabin, has a boat, or even if they've posted nice vacation photos on Facebook. Get the idea? Now it's your turn.

Remember, keep it simple. Keep your target market in mind. Everything you write down needs to be directly connected to your perfect client. If you make it easy, people will notice these things without any effort and - BINGO! - you'll be top of mind.

ACTION

List the things that your clients, COIs, and friends can SEE, NOTICE or OBSERVE that might be an indicator that someone could be a good prospect for you. You'll want to keep track of this list because it will come in handy soon.

Congrats! You're taking the lead nicely in developing the plays for your playbook. The pieces of your education process are coming together. Now you have the clarity to describe your perfect client. On top of that, you have a list of things that others can be looking out for on your behalf.

We're not done yet. There's even more...

Let's engage more of the senses. People talk, and a lot of people complain to almost anyone who will listen. You know these folks, and you can bet your clients and COIs know them, too. Now we need you to make a list of those complaints or statements that your prospects are out there making every day. Why? Because we want your clients, COIs, and friends to recognize that when they hear one of these statements or complaints, they should think of you!

Let's give you some examples. Perhaps someone is out there saying, "It scares me not knowing if I have enough money to retire" OR "I can't stand my husband any longer. I'm filing for a divorce."

The key to this exercise is to write the statement in the actual words of the prospect, NOT your words. Put yourself in the shoes of your clients or COIs. What might some of their friends be saying?

Let's see what you can come up with this time.

ACTION

Make a list of at least 4-5 complaints or statements that people might be expressing that your referral sources might HEAR. Be sure to capture their actual words exactly and not put your own jargon in by remote control.

Almost done. There are just a few more things to consider.

When one of your clients, COIs, or friends has recognized an opportunity for you, often they just don't know how to bring you up in conversation. They simply don't know what to say. As a leader when it comes to educating your network, your role is to help your clients, friends and COIs be successful at referring you, especially since we already know they want to. We find that when you give people a few good questions to ask others, it opens up a lot of conversations and typically generates many more opportunities for you.

For example, this is the scenario you're striving for – your client hears a potential prospect say:

Prospect: "It scares me not knowing if I have enough money to retire."

Client: "Who do you have helping you with that?"

Prospect: "No one. I don't trust financial advisors."

Client: "I trust my advisor. Would you like to meet her?"

Prospect: "Well, ok. If YOU like her she's probably good."

Most scenarios end here with the client giving the prospect your business card and saying something like, "Here's her card, you should give her a call."

That's not what you want to happen. Instead, this is the better scenario.

Client: "Great! What's the best way for her to reach you? I can have her call you tomorrow."

This kind of interaction will not happen naturally; it won't happen without your leadership. Instead, it will quickly head in the direction mentioned above where the client (or COI) merely passes along your information. All too often, you never even know this conversation happened.

Our goal here is for you to raise the bar. By raising the bar and teaching people how to refer you in the best possible way, more clients and COIs will be successful in bringing you people who really do need and want your help. From there, human nature takes over because if they experience success at referring you, they are likely to refer you again.

ACTION

What other good questions do your clients need to have top of mind to help them open up a conversation? Write down those questions, and if you really feel adventurous, create a scenario like the one above to round out your questions.

As a quick review, here is a series of questions that you should be able to answer for yourself before sharing them with (or educating) others on how to refer you.

☐ Who specifically are you looking for as your client?

☐ What are some personal characteristics that you prefer in your favorite clients?

☐ What are visual or audio triggers or clues that someone else might see, hear, or notice that would indicate they need your help?

☐ What are your prospects complaining about that someone else might hear?

- ☐ What are easy questions that someone might ask a friend to determine if they need you?
- ☐ What do you want someone to say about you?
- ☐ What **don't** you want someone to say about you?

By now you might be saying, "WOW! This is a lot of information! Do my clients and COIs really need to know all of this?" The simple answer is YES. Look at what's happening now when they don't have this insight. When you take some time to actually teach people how to refer you with this kind of information, guess what happens? You get referred! But honestly, this does not come easily for a lot of women advisors. That's why we have tailored our coaching process to support your efforts in getting the results you want.

The real question now is what do you do with all of this information?

The best thing to do is to consolidate it so that it fits onto one sheet of paper. More than a single page is too much. When working to educate your clients, the objective is to share this information with your clients in a meeting dedicated to talking about who they might know that should know about you and your specialties. Yes, that's right. A SEPARATE meeting, NOT during a client review meeting. Talking about referrals during a review meeting is a man's way. We believe that the reason this often feels uncomfortable to YOU is that it's not YOUR way.

You know that the review meeting is intended to be all about the client, not about you. So instead of breaching this protocol, imagine taking your clients out to lunch, or maybe coffee, or even meeting at their house. The point is to dedicate time to talking about referrals and to give your referral process the much-deserved time necessary to represent its significance.

When working to educate your COIs, you want to do something very similar. Ask if they would be open to meeting for lunch because you have some updated information about your business that you would appreciate sharing. When you meet, be sure to take two copies of your information, one for you and one for the COI to take away. Take your time to review each component we've discussed and encourage your COI to ask questions for clarification. For many, sharing this information feels best if it happens over several meetings. That's ok too. The bottom line is to share your insight and client preference and educate those who can and should be referring you.

These are the kinds of conversations we coach our clients through to help them gain confidence, comfort, skill, and ultimately results. Almost 100% of the time, our clients are surprised at the reactions they receive when they share this kind of information with COIs, clients, and friends. An open dialogue like this will trigger many more opportunities for you. You will leave these meetings adding prospects into your pipeline and knowing that you have engaged your network in your referral process. In order for this to be a true system, however, you must work to duplicate it over and over again and learn to add a level of finesse based on a person's behavioral style. (Behavioral style? What's that, you ask? That's a big topic reserved for another book.) Then you'll need to develop your follow-up system to support the new business activity that will be generated by your engagement.

So far, we've helped you become very strategic about with whom you spend your time since we intend for you to get the most bang for your buck in every hour spent with great COIs.

We've helped you to clarify your niche or target market and who you want as clients, intentionally leaving doubt and confusion behind.

We've helped you develop language for teaching clients and COIs how to refer you, intentionally triggering opportunities to enable you to help more people.

And, we've shown you how to intentionally leverage the many people in your network by educating them on how they can best refer you. *Everything we do is intentional.* Now it's time to take an intentional deep dive into how you specifically ask for referrals in a manner that makes you comfortable and gets results.

SECTION 5

Lead Your Referrals

"You get in life what you have the courage to ask for."
- Oprah Winfrey

We've finally arrived at the big, heavy topic of specifically ASKING for referrals. If you're not a fan of asking, take a deep breath. Asking is not really that hard to do. The hard part is getting the negative self-talk out of your head that's stopping you from asking.

Most of what you've probably learned about asking for referrals came from watching others do it, most likely male advisors. Typically, men have no problem asking for referrals (although that's not always the case). Most men tend to be direct and don't let rejection impact their self-esteem. Perhaps what you've learned or observed about asking for referrals doesn't resonate with you or feel comfortable to you. No surprise.

Women fear damaging their relationships, and they worry that clients will leave if they ask them for referrals. Many women advisors we spoke to simply don't want to bother others. The problem is, most women haven't yet found their own way to ask for referrals. And as mentioned earlier, most of the women advisors we've worked with struggle with promoting themselves in a comfortable way. Some of the things we typically hear are:

- "I hate to bother people."
- "I don't want to sound desperate."
- "They're too busy to worry about me."
- "I don't want to be pushy or sound salesy."
- "I don't want to make someone feel uncomfortable."

So female advisors often remain quiet, ever hopeful that if they do great work for their clients they will be referred.

Maybe you're like our client Tina who as a young advisor observed a male senior advisor hammering a client for referrals at the end of a review meeting. She observed how uncomfortable the client appeared and vowed never to put her clients in that position. She knew that pounding method did not resonate with her; however, she did not know of any other way to ask for referrals. It wasn't until we coached together that she gained comfort in asking for referrals by creating her own approach. There is never just one solution for asking for referrals. The best solution is the one that feels good for both you and your client (or whomever you might be asking).

The reality is that over time, like Tina, you have trained your brain to believe that asking for referrals is scary, hard, and painful. Did you know that one of your brain's primary roles is to keep you safe? If your brain senses that you're about to do something scary, it will remind you that this is not a safe activity. Consequently, you avoid the activity of asking.

What we need to do is actually retrain your brain to believe that asking is not hard, that it's ok, and that it's safe. Your brain can and will literally create new wiring for this activity. Before you know it, when you are about to ask for referrals, your brain will relax and say, 'Oh that's right, this is ok now; we're safe' and you are free to move about the country in relaxation.

This might sound funny to you, but sometimes the first thing we need to do is to tell ourselves over and over that asking for referrals is ok. **The key is that you truly have to believe it.** Believe that people really do want to help you. Believe that when your clients say how much they love you, they really do love you. Believe that once you've found the right COIs, they too will want to help you succeed. Believe that when you ask, you will receive.

If you find yourself getting worried about asking, plant these few words in your head *"It is simple. It is not hard.*

It will be fun." Repeating them over and over will help your brain to rewire itself.

The second thing we need to do is predetermine your success by asking the right people. You can't expect to get referrals from everyone, but you can certainly increase your chances by asking the right people. Who are the right people? Based on our experience, we would recommend that you start with this list:

- People who have referred you in the past
- People who have told you they would refer you
- People who have told you they love you (or some variation of that)
- Your favorite people, favorite clients, best friends, travel buddies, etc.

A big part of getting past your fear and retraining your brain is experiencing success. You WILL experience success when you ask these people in your life. These are the people who would help you in any way they can. And you've probably never asked them to help you...yet. Another client, Claire, witnessed this first hand. She approached her best friends to ask them for referrals. In fact, she shared a lot of the information we developed earlier in the book with her friends. When she told them that she was afraid to ask them they said, "Are you kidding us! Of course, we'll help you!"

As we mentioned, there are quite a few different ways to ask for referrals. Some ways are passive and others are more engaging. You're looking for two things: comfort and effectiveness. Passively asking for referrals might feel comfortable because it keeps you safe. But it doesn't produce steady, predictable results. These strategies rely on someone else taking action and often without you knowing it. A passive request at least lets people know you're looking for new business and gently reminds them to think of you, but it's not directed towards a specific relationship. Passive approaches typically mean that everyone gets the same message. There are always pros and cons to any method.

Here are a few examples of different ways to passively ask for referrals. Of course, always remember, you may need to run things by your compliance officer.

PASSIVELY asking for referrals

Email signature & business cards – You may have already seen an email signature or the back of other advisors' business cards a statement like "The best compliment I can receive is a referral." This plants a seed (even if only for a brief second) that referrals are meaningful for you. This passive message lets people know that you are accepting referrals and open to their introductions.

Signage – We've seen financial advisor firms use signage in different ways too. Sometimes there might be a sign in the office placed strategically near the exit door that says, "We appreciate your referrals." Another client once put an 8x10 frame on his credenza facing outward so the client could see it while sitting at his desk. Inside the frame, he used a statement made popular by Mark Sheer in his book, *Referrals* that read, "Who do you know who needs to know about the work we do?" Incidentally, this phrase, "I am expanding my business and I need your help. Who do you know who" has been studied. As Mark points out in his book, this phrase is the number one phrase that produces the most referrals. All you need to do is figure out how you want to end that phrase to spark interest. For example, "who do you know who is getting divorced" or *"who do you know who* just received an inheritance?" Think of all the different endings you could add to that statement. Think of how many other ways you could apply this statement as well.

Client Onboarding – It's fairly common for financial advisors to have an onboarding process for new clients. Many women advisors we know give out a packet of information to new clients. Inside many of our clients' packets, you'll find at least one sheet that highlights how referrals are valued by their firm. We know successful women advisors who specifically honor clients who refer to their firm. If they have a special program to support client referrals, a description of that referral program is included in this packet as well. If you're not doing this already, maybe there's a way for you to include something on referrals in your onboarding process going forward.

Sending a letter, card, or newsletter – This strategy is a combination of passively and actively asking for referrals. It's passive because you send it off in the mail or through email, and you never know if the client will open it or if they will take the time to read it. It's active because it involves you creating the language for that letter, card, or newsletter.

Some advisors will incorporate the "who do you know" statements in their letter and/or newsletter. Others will include the statement "The best compliment I can receive is a referral" not only on their business card but in their newsletter as well. Some advisors prefer to send a card or invitation to remind clients of an upcoming event while encouraging them to bring a guest.

We could probably go on and on about passively asking for referrals but you see the direction this is headed. All of these strategies could be a part of your passive referral process and will accomplish a certain level of awareness and activity. But to really have an impact on your referral results and engage your network, you've got to lead the process by actively asking. Let's take a look at several different ways to actively ask your network (not just your clients) for referrals and various tools you can use.

Remember: *"It is simple. It is not hard. It will be fun."*

ACTIVELY asking for referrals

Sit-down 1:1 meeting - As mentioned earlier, engaging people in a sit-down meeting to educate them on how to refer you is a very proactive, focused approach to introducing your referral process. It never fails that when you're reviewing the information that you've pulled together regarding your ideal client, what to listen and look for, and so on, the person sitting across from you (client, COI, best friend, yoga buddy, etc.) will automatically start thinking of people that match the description you're sharing. They will think of people they know who are having the experiences you describe. They will remember hearing someone say the very statement you just reviewed with them. It's uncanny – and it really works. Sometimes, they even hear or see themselves reflected in your description and say to you, "Hey, maybe we should talk."

The most important thing to remember at this stage is that by starting with your best people first, you gain more comfort. How do you get your best friend to sit down with you to talk about your practice? Call her up and say, "Sally, I've been working on something incredible for my business. Would you be open to having lunch or dinner with me so I can share it with you?" Why would she say anything other than "Yes!"? And when you're actually meeting with her and walking her through the information, if you feel the need, all you have to do is ask her, "Who do you know who's like this?" Success resides in actively asking for referrals!

Asking at an event – Imagine holding a special event for your clients. It could be a presentation from one of your COIs, a cooking demonstration, a wine tasting class, the opportunities are endless. These client events are very popular. The thing to keep in mind here is that you have an engaged, captive audience with a lot of people who think you're wonderful.

If you've done one of these before, did you leverage the opportunity to ask your clients for referrals? The question is, how can you do this comfortably for everyone? Remember your list of favorite clients who have referred you before? If one of those folks is planning to attend, ask that client if she or he would take a couple minutes to share the story of how and why they referred their best friend to you. Don't over think it or make it difficult. They'll be very happy to help out.

"It is simple. It is not hard. It will be fun."

Your favorite clients are always happy to help. If that doesn't work or you're just not feeling ready to ask for help this way, take it upon yourself to discuss referrals with your audience. When you're talking about your firm, you can use a few different approaches.

Leverage their experience – Say to the audience, "Most of you here have been connected to us by someone else. Please stand if you were. Thank you! Someone you care about introduced you to us. You've experienced what it's like to become a part of our family. We would be honored to help the people you care most about as well."

Leverage common life situation – Say to the audience, "Most of you here came to us because you needed to know for certain that you would not outlive your money. Who do you know who is worried about the same thing? We would love to meet them for lunch or coffee."

Leverage a desire to help – Say to the audience, "We want you to know that our goal this year is to get 10 new clients who are just like you. We would love your help in meeting people like you who need to know about the work we do. If you have someone in mind, please call me to talk further and perhaps we can all go out to lunch or dinner together."

Take a close look at the language in these approaches. We never even mention the word 'referral.' Why? It's not necessary. Focus on giving your clients the opportunity to HELP the people they care about most by connecting them to you.

Lead by Leveraging LinkedIn

Do you have a LinkedIn account? The bigger question is: do you use it, and if so, how do you use it?

Most likely you have an account and probably have more than 100 connections. It's likely that many of you reading this have many, many connections. However, a lot of women advisors simply just don't know what to do with LinkedIn or more importantly how to leverage it. Too many advisors have told us they shy away from social media of any kind because of compliance.

The best way we can help you leverage your network on LinkedIn doesn't really have to involve compliance. But you do need to have access to the Premium Sales version of LinkedIn to truly leverage the network. As of this writing, LinkedIn requires you to purchase a Premium version in order to sort through your connections' connections to see who you would like to meet. The sales version currently runs about $60-$70/month and is quite effective for our strategy. (We are not affiliated in any way with LinkedIn.)

Imagine if you could see the connections of all the people you know. Finally, you could literally see that your fitness coach is connected to the CEO of ABC Company and you've been trying to get into ABC Company for months to evaluate their 401K plan. This LinkedIn upgrade could no doubt lead you to a few new opportunities, prospects, and possible referrals, right? Enter LinkedIn (Premium). With the help of this tool, you no longer need to wait for your network members to have a referral fall into their lap before something happens. You can now lead this referral process very proactively.

Here's how we'd like you to leverage your connections on LinkedIn using our very own S.I.F.T. Method™ without ever worrying about compliance. The S.I.F.T. Method™ stands for:

Schedule
Invite
Focus
Track

The first step is to SCHEDULE. LinkedIn represents a network. As with any group of people you know, if you want to engage in networking with them, you have to commit some time to it. If you belong to an association network, you have to commit time to networking with that group of people to attain any results, right? The same is true for LinkedIn. We want you to think of networking on LinkedIn in the same way you think of networking with a chamber or any other physical network. Set time aside on your calendar for networking LinkedIn just as if you were setting time aside to go to an event. In general, 1 hour per week is sufficient compared to what you're probably doing right now. During that 1 hour per week, you'll be implementing one or more of the other three steps.

The second step is to INVITE. Concentrate on growing the number of LinkedIn connections you have right now. Some think the bigger your network, the more possibilities you have waiting for you. We agree, to a point. However, the better your relationship with each of your network members, the more possibilities there will be for the kind of engagement you'll need to actively generate referrals.

Set a goal for yourself. Invite 10 people per week to connect with you on LinkedIn. That's 520 people per year if you stick with it! Invite every new person you meet when networking. Invite mentors and work colleagues from the past. Look for neighbors that you used to live next to previously. Create a new habit to invite people regularly. We suggest that you invite people you know or have met, not people who simply show up as someone you should connect to randomly through LinkedIn's algorithms. Sticking to people you know builds a more robust list of connections that you can then research at a later time, feeling relatively confident that when you reach out to those people with a request, they will respond to you.

The third step is FOCUS. When you focus, you get more. It doesn't matter what you focus on. The fact is, when you focus, you get more of what you're focusing on. Period.

This works in all aspects of your life. For example, when you focus (negatively) on your weight, you gain more weight. When you focus on your aches and pains, you get more aches and pains. When you focus on money, you get more money. When you focus on being happy, you get more happiness.

While you are S.I.F.T.ing through LinkedIn, we are going to ask you to begin searching your connections, FOCUSing on one person at a time, someone you know well. The goal of this step is to create a list of people you wish to meet or be introduced to with the help of one of your LinkedIn connections. Once you have that list generated, you'll ask for help from your LinkedIn connection by discussing the list with them in person or over the phone.

Start by clicking on the connections of one of your favorite LinkedIn peeps. In order to simplify this search, you need to know what focus filters you want to apply to help you sort more effectively. It might be good to reference your information on your target market description when entering your filters. Depending on your target market, some sample focus filters could be

"CEO" or "owner" or "company name" or "PhD" or "Medical."

Remember, you will get more of what you focus on.

It all depends on what you're looking for. This is an example of when that niche concept can really expand your opportunities. If you are looking to serve doctors, you will use the appropriate filters to search for connections that are doctors.

Once you see who your LinkedIn peep knows that match your search, select who you want to meet and start a list. It's best to keep this list to around 6-10 people to discuss at any one time. Certainly, less than this is equally effective. Remember, your LinkedIn peeps will not necessarily know all of their connections on LinkedIn, so your list will not be 100% fruitful. Over the years, we have all accepted offers to connect with people without knowing the person personally.

Think of this LinkedIn method as proactively cherry-picking your prospects to fill your pipeline. It doesn't get much better than that. If you work your LinkedIn network by looking through 3-5 people's connections each week, you will build quite a list of potential "warm" prospects. So how do you use this list you've created?

The fourth step is TRACK. Tracking involves several mini-steps, including the most important one: the ask. Reminder: *"It is simple. It is not hard. It will be fun."*

Now that you have a list of people that you'd like to meet from your contact's connections, call or email your LinkedIn peep to meet in person or talk on the phone. Here's an example of what you could say:

> "Hi Jen. I was searching through your connections on LinkedIn, and I discovered several people that I would like to discuss with you. Would you be available to meet me for coffee or lunch to talk about them further?"

During your lunch with Jen, start by reviewing the list to see who Jen knows well enough that she feels comfortable introducing you. As we said earlier, the reality is that many people link with everyone who requests a connection, so sometimes your list of 10 people you want to meet quickly boils down to 5 or 6 people your contact actually knows. That's OK. That means there are 5 or 6 people Jen could potentially introduce or connect you to that you know match your target market profile.

Once you narrow the list down to the people Jen can introduce you to, you can begin to strategize the best way to make that introduction.

For example, would it be best for you to craft an email so that Jen can pass it along to this person on your behalf? Do you have an event coming up that Jen can invite these people to so they can meet you in person? Would it be possible for Jen to organize a lunch meeting? Create the process together so that everyone feels comfortable and you make it easy for Jen to be successful at following up.

Then finally, track the plan so that you can follow up appropriately.

The S.I.F.T. Method™ works very well and if you notice, you shouldn't need to worry about compliance. All you need is to carve out the time to work the LinkedIn network and build up your LinkedIn connections so that you have a network to browse. It's a place where you can proactively reach out to your friends to see if they will help introduce you to the people they know. The most important part of this strategy is making the connecting process easy for your friends and business colleagues. When you apply this strategy consistently, you will see just how willing your network is to help you.

We know the real struggles with asking, and we also know how to help advisors move beyond these hurdles. If you're still hesitant or doubtful, think of the process this way: Why do we refer people to someone we know? Usually because those people need help, and we know and trust someone else who can help them. How does it feel when you refer someone to a friend who can help? Pretty good, right? It feels good to help out two people; the person you referred to and the person being referred. You connected these two people because you believed in your friend and knew she or he would do a good job. Exactly! What a great feeling!

We never want you to deny your clients, COIs, friends, and neighbors that same good feeling of being able to help someone they care about by sending that person to you. Leading your network requires you to lead the way so that others will follow. Your leadership skills activate the law of reciprocity and engage your network to produce greater results for everyone involved in the process. All it takes to be the leader of your network is your willingness to teach other people (clients, COIs – and don't stop there, include your friends, neighbors, and family too) how to refer you and your ability to make it a simple, easy, comfortable process for all involved, including you! Let's act on this now.

ACTION

Ask for referrals

This one is simply written. There are many strategies here to help you ask for referrals. Some are passive and some are active. Choose something here that you feel ready to implement. Maybe you're ready to stretch yourself a little. The main objective is forward motion, trust that your relationships are open to helping you and ask.

We repeat: *"It is simple. It is not hard. It will be fun."*

SECTION 6

Best Advice – Woman to Woman

"Behind every successful woman is a tribe
of other successful women who have her back."
-Anonymous

We felt strongly that this book needed to contain the voices of women advisors from across the country. We heard their frustrations, their stories, their lessons, their struggles, their opinions, and their successes. Most importantly, we felt that it was essential for these successful woman advisors to share their personal tips and advice to help other female advisors succeed.

As you read through these words of wisdom, regardless of how long you've been in this profession, you will be moved and inspired by your sisters. You will be reminded of some things that you've forgotten or get charged up to do something you know you've needed to do. You will feel a sense of solidarity. Our vision is to create a community of women advisors supporting each other along their journeys. These words represent the beginning of that supportive female community of *A Woman's Way.*

The final question in our survey of women advisors was:

> **What would be the one thing you've learned that you would share with a younger woman advisor to help her succeed?**

As we listened, we heard some common themes. We encourage you to pay attention to the voices of women in your community.

Be YOU!

- Speak up! Every woman generation is better than the last.

- Do what you're comfortable with.

- Find your authentic self.

- Find what you're really passionate about and follow it.

- Align YOU with your mind, your voice, and your passion.

- Center yourself on things that bring you joy.

- Really try to figure out what your personal strengths are and build a career around those from the beginning.

- Have a vision of yourself, your practice, and where you want to take it.

- Know who you are and what you want to accomplish.

- It's ok to change your vision as you grow.

- Lead with your passion and be very authentic.

- Don't try to be anyone else.

- If it doesn't feel right, don't do it.

- Lots of successful women advisors create it themselves – create your vision.

- Be true to yourself. You won't fit a square peg into a round hole. Be natural and it will serve you well.

- Stay true to yourself! It's not about selling a product.

- Be real. Be likable. People work with people they truly like.

- Capitalize on your assets and the fact that you are a woman in a man's world.

Find Support!

- Find a mentor – someone you admire.

- Partner with someone who is good at something you're not.
- Find a mentor and find personal freedom.
- Ask for help.
- Realize that one person doesn't know everything--cut yourself some slack.
- Get a mentor! Man or woman, someone who understands stocks and bonds and the business as a whole. Someone who has a passion for what you want.
- Find an advocate.
- FIND A MENTOR! This is the key to starting out and getting a fast start.
- Ask someone to hold you accountable.
- Find someone you can share successes and disappointments with early on.
- Find mentors or cheerleaders in the industry.
- Get honest feedback.
- I will challenge other women advisors to step into leadership roles because other women advisors need to see you there. Be the change you seek and it will evolve change.
- It's all about finding someone to take you under their wing and guide you through their experience. It's ok to be a fly on the wall to see how another advisor (mentor) handles it.

- Make sure you have a support group or mentor you report to all the time. Accountability! Two heads are better than one.

- Find a really good mentor - male or female - who can guide you through the process, explain CFP®, excite you about the industry.

- Find a good mentor and work at a company that treats all advisors the same and respects women.

Build a Network!

- Start to build your peer network NOW!
- Get started. Build relationships early.
- Network, network, network.
- Get involved in some industry groups.
- You need people around you; don't do it alone.
- Find others who are like you.
- Lean on resources to know things you don't (wholesalers, FPA, etc.).
- Don't be afraid to break out of the old boy's network.

Be Client Centered!

- Think about what the client would do or feel first.
- Client's perspective is always #1.

- Think about the client first.
- Always do the right thing for the client – nothing else matters – regardless of how much you get paid – or it will surely blow up in your face.
- Look at your clients as if they are your own family.
- Do it for them and yourself.

Stand Tall!

- Conduct yourself professionally.
- Be confident that your work is good enough!
- Forget you're a woman. There are NO barriers. You are competent. Your expectation should be that "I have a right to be at the table."
- Don't be intimidated by strengths.
- Look and act like a successful advisor.
- Look and act like the position you WANT to have.
- Be consistent in your demeanor and behavior.
- Stand up for yourself. Nobody will do it for you.
- Be more confident in yourself, no matter what!
- Always be aware of handling yourself respectably in public.
- Fake it till you make it. Be confident that your ideas matter.

Business Advice!

- Keep overhead low.

- Stay focused.

- Set five goals each year with a couple of easy ones and a couple to carry over to next year.

- Take the risk and learn the business early on.

- Be the master of your own destiny!

- Know it will be a roller coaster ride day-to-day. You need to keep the highs and lows steady.

- Enjoy the baby steps.

- Find your niche.

- You don't have to be a man to be successful.

- You may not know everything at the beginning.

- Do your research when you don't know something; speak your voice; see yourself as valuable.

- Find a niche, learn everything about it, and be able to solve their problems – you will get business.

- Become the go-to expert in that niche.

- Be willing to do a lot without getting paid – articles, speaking, networking, etc.

- Be kind to yourself and don't give up!

- Don't run from it; learn a lot; put your boots on and go someplace where you are appreciated.

- This is an ever-lasting learning process. You will continue to learn because every client is different.

- Align with a successful advisor for at least the first 2-3 years.

- Lots of unknowns. Be an expert. Stay up to speed.

- Don't focus on what can go wrong but rather the positive side.

- There are only 3 things you have to do in this business: activity, activity, activity. Be in front of more people to sell more stuff.

- You can control who becomes your client and you can control who you ask.

- Be prepared for any opportunity.

- You may need to be your co-worker's boss later, so act consistently.

Work/Life Balance!

- Know this industry is VERY flexible.
- You CAN achieve work/life balance as an FA.
- Yes, you can have it all.
- It's a great career for a woman. Don't be afraid.
- This should not feel like work.

ACTION

Go back through this list and circle the advice that resonates with you the most. Write these items down in a journal or type them into a document or app that you like and look at them often. Be sure that no matter where you put it, you will have access to this list daily.

Now, add your own answers to the question ...

> **What would be the one thing you've learned that you would share with another woman advisor to help her succeed?**

Allow these words, your own words and what you've learned from this book, to act as your compass guiding you forward while evolving your practice *A Woman's Way*. Equipped with your internal fortitude and the strength of this sisterhood, creating a practice that truly resonates with your authentic self is not only possible but absolutely essential.

SECTION 7

So, what's next?

*"The future belongs to those who
believe in the beauty of their dreams."*
– Eleanor Roosevelt

Let's check in …

How are you feeling right now? Are you feeling empowered? Our hope is that you are feeling excited and validated that yes, you can leverage your strengths as a woman to have the kind of practice you've always dreamed of creating because YES. YOU. CAN.

This is not a rah-rah book to cheer you up. We've seen big change and bigger success happen time and again with our clients using the same information contained in this book.

Yes, there are significant external hurdles to overcome while reaching for your success (as mentioned in Section One). These are the systemic challenges that currently come with the territory. It's hard to escape the fact that you are working hard to thrive in a male-dominated profession. You also can't deny the fact that the wealth management profession is poorly rated when it comes to gender equity in pay. It's shocking to see that a *SourceMedia Research* survey as recent as March 2018 listed wealth management as the industry with the highest prevalence of sexual harassment. Gender bias and discrimination are still very much in the culture of many firms and wirehouses. Work/life balancing beams, despite the efforts to promote flexibility, have not gotten much smaller over the years.

External barriers are real. The profession has a lot of work to do to eliminate these barriers in order to create more welcoming cultures for women advisors. This book, unfortunately, cannot lift the veil entirely off these issues on behalf of all women advisors. Our hope here is to, at the very least, lift the veil enough to expose the inequities and validate what women in wealth management are still experiencing today.

We want those with decision-making abilities to see and hear the truth within these pages and commit to creating new, inclusive cultures that ultimately attract more women. Our hope for you as a woman advisor is that by reading this book, you will gain more empowerment, confidence, and fortitude to push forward by you simply being you. We want you to be prouder than ever of who you are and tap deeper into your personal inner strength.

We see that inner strength lifting your voice and building a much-needed support network for all women in wealth management.

We intend to continue doing our part by drawing attention to these external barriers and encouraging the profession to respond more thoroughly with positive change. However, as we mentioned throughout the book, there are a number of *internal* barriers that put up resistance for you as well, and these inner obstacles are fully and immediately within your control.

Remember those negative voices and beliefs that travel up into your brain and sabotage you? These are the little devils on your shoulder that keep you from asking for referrals or cause you to doubt the strength of your relationships. They're the ones who keep your expectations low because you don't feel worthy enough to ask for referrals or that stop you from asking for help because you don't want to bother people. What have you done with your little devils? Are they still there? Are they as loud as they used to be? Have you sent any of them on a permanent vacation yet?

And what about those unproductive behaviors that get in the way of your progress? Many of these behaviors have become bad habits. Unfortunately, these bad habits can cost you success if you're not careful. Believing that you must be the one to say 'yes' will always steal time from another aspect of your life. Not being comfortable with receiving can stop an enormous amount of good from coming in your direction. Striving for perfection will ultimately chip away at your confidence and self-esteem. Allowing time suckers to rule your day steals your productivity. And ignoring your needs and values will set yourself up for frustration, exhaustion, dismay, and maybe even depression. And not asking for referrals leaves a lot of money on the table.

Some of you reading this book will want to change everything all at once. Others will feel that you have quite a few of these things under control, but you know deep down that there is still room for improvement in some areas. We recommend that you approach what you want to change as if you were eating that elephant mentioned earlier – one bite at a time.

Begin by finding the one thing that you really want to tackle first. Zero in on it. Focus your energy on it. Remember, that which gets your focus will grow and change. Be intentional. Set goals. Once you have determined a goal, you need discipline, accountability, and the right activity to make it happen. As a leader, you have to be intentional. Everything you do should be intentional. You should leave nothing to chance. That's what followers do. They leave everything to chance. If you read between the lines throughout this book, you'll notice that everything is intentional.

When you feel you are making good progress and can dig into the next internal barrier, go for it. The point is to focus. Don't try to do everything at once.

We want every female financial advisor reading this book to become wildly successful and ultimately become a role model. The more women who succeed by embracing their natural strengths as women to build flourishing practices and firms, the more and more role models will be created for the future. Women on the outside looking in as they consider this career will see themselves reflected back experiencing the kind of success they want without compromising who they are in the process.

Does the industry have work to do to build a more inviting and supportive culture for women advisors? Absolutely, no doubt. This transformation will involve systemic change, and change starts today.

Our focus is on developing YOU and other women advisors like you who want to shine like a beacon beyond the sea of black suits. We see you as the red boat on the cover of this book, never fearful of being who you are and flourishing with your extraordinary natural talents. Yes, it is important for you to *authentically* build the practice you dream of, but it is equally important for you to help pave the way for those who will come behind you, just as those ahead have done for you.

FINAL ACTION

Be grateful for those who have offered you the inspiration and support that has lifted you to where you are today.

Be grateful for the mentors yet to enter your life.

Live by the words that have touched you and savor them so you can share when you become a future mentor.

Establish your goals for moving forward in creating your practice *A Woman's Way*. Take some time to think through what you've learned and create your plan for implementation.

Now, reach out to a younger advisor and offer her your support. After all, authenticity and sisterhood are at the core of *A Woman's Way*.

> *"I do not wish women to have power*
> *over men; but over themselves."*
> *-Mary Shelley*

MY PLAN

Bibliography

Books

Covey, Steven. *The Seven Habits of Highly Effective People*. New York, NY: Simon & Schuster, 1989.

Kay, Katty and Claire Shipman. *The Confidence Code*. New York, NY: HarperCollins Publishers, 2014.

Kreamer, Patty. *But I Might Need It Someday*. Pittsburgh, PA: Publish Connect, 2002.

Kreamer, Patty. *The Power of Simplicity*. Pittsburgh, PA: Publish Connect, 2004.

Maxwell, John C. *Developing the Leader Within You*. Nashville, TN: Thomas Nelson, 1993.

Misner, Ivan R., PhD and Michelle R. Donovan. *The 29% Solution: 52 Weekly Networking Success Strategies*. Austin, TX: Greenleaf Publishing, 2008.

Sheer, Mark. *Referrals: Reap Rewards, Earn More Money in Less Time and Have More Fun*. M. Sheer Seminars, 1993.

Spira, Jonathan. *Overload! How Too Much Information Is Hazardous to Your Organization*. Hoboken, New Jersey: John Wiley & Sons, Inc., 2011.

Additional Resources

SECTION ONE

2017 Adviser Compensation and Staffing Study, *Investment News*, September 11, 2017, http://www.investmentnews.com/dcce/20170911/4/4/wp_sponsored/3471669.

CFP® Board WIN Initiative, "Making More Room for Women in the Financial Planning Profession," Certified Financial Planner Board of Standards, Inc., 2014.

Fischer, Erin McKelle. "Which industries have the worst gender pay gap? New census data reveals where wage equality suffers the most," *Bustle.com*, https://www.bustle.com/articles/70724-which-industries-have-the-worst-gender-pay-gap-new-census-data-reveals-where-wage-equality-suffers.

Ford, Erinn. "3 Ways to Close the Gender Gap Among Advisors," *Financial Planning*; June 18, 2015, http://www.financial-planning.com/blogs/3-ways-to-close-the-gender-gap-among-advisors-2693232-1.html?zkPrintable=1&nopagination=1.

Gilbere, Gloria PhD. "Female Friendship Good for Your Health," *Total Health Magazine*; October 22, 2013, http://totalhealthmagazine.com/Lifestyle/Female-Friendship-Good-for-Your-Health.html.

Gleeson, Jerry. "Wells Fargo Settles Sex Discrimination Claims For $32 Million,"
Wealth Management Magazine; February 25, 2011, http://wealthmanagement.com/practice-management/wells-fargo-settles-sex-discrimination-claims-32-million.

Kamen, Dr. Randy. "A Compelling Argument About Why Women Need Friendships,"
Huffpost Women, November 29, 2012, http://www.huffingtonpost.com/randy-kamen-gredinger-edd/female-friendship_b_2193062.html.

Kauflin, Jeff. "The 10 Industries with the Biggest Gender Pay Gaps," *Forbes.com*, December 6, 2016, https://www.forbes.com/sites/jeffkauflin/2016/12/06/the-10-industries-with-the-biggest-gender-pay-gaps/#3629e1fb51d4.

Miko, Leighmann. "Want More Women Advisors,"
Financial Advisor Magazine, March 1, 2018, https://www.fa-mag.com/news/want-more-women-advisors-37366.html?section=47.

Practice Management Group of State Street Global Advisors and InvestmentNews Research, "Women in Advice: Inspiring the Next Generation of Financial Advisors," *InvestmentNews*, February 9, 2018, http://www.investmentnews.com/article/20180209/FREE/180109988/investmentnews-research-and-state-street-global-advisors-release-new.

Welsch, Andrew. "Wealth management fares worst in broad study of sexual harassment," *Financial Planning*, March 12, 2018, https://www.financial-planning.com/news/wealth-managements-problem-with-sexual-harassment-in-the-workplace.

SECTION TWO

Gross, Dr. Gail. "How Men and Women Handle Stress Differently." *HuffingtonPost.com*, November 14, 2016; www.huffingtonpost.com/entry/how-men-and-women-handle-stress-differently_us_58236ec5e4b0334571e0a4cd.

Kahler, Rick. "4 Qualities a Financial Advisor Ought to Have," *Time Inc. Network*, June 30, 2015, http://time.com/money/3882506/financial-adviser-qualities.

Ma, Roger. "5 Things to Look for When Picking a Financial Advisor," *Forbes.com*, January 4, 2017, https://www.forbes.com/sites/rogerma/2017/01/04/5-things-to-look-for-when-picking-a-financial-advisor/#598180b01fc4.

SECTION THREE

Gorlick, Adam. "Media multitaskers pay mental price," *Stanford News*, August 24, 2009, http://news.stanford.edu/2009/08/24/multitask-research-study-082409/.

Schulte, Brigid. "Work interruptions can cost you 6 hours a day. An efficiency expert explains how to avoid them," *Washington Post*, June 1, 2015, https://www.washingtonpost.com/news/inspired-life/wp/2015/06/01/interruptions-at-work-can-cost-you-up-to-6-hours-a-day-heres-how-to-avoid-them/?utm_term=.76a3a6997b21.

Weinschenk, Susan PhD. "The True Cost of Multi-Tasking," *Psychology Today*, September 18, 2012, https://www.psychologytoday.com/blog/brain-wise/201209/the-true-cost-multi-tasking.

SECTION FOUR

Financial Planning Association, "Drivers of Business Growth Study", *FPA Research & Practice Institute*, 2014, https://www.onefpa.org/business-success/ResearchandPracticeInstitute/Documents/FPA_RPI_quarterly%20report_R5.pdf.

Littlechild, Julie. "Why Do So Few Clients Actually Refer?" Julie Littlechild's Blog, April 4, 2018, https://www.absoluteengagement.com/blog/growth/why-dont-clients-refer/.

Michelle R. Donovan is known for her ability to help our clients gain focus and hold them accountable to achieve exceptional results. As a referral & business coach, Michelle has helped many financial firms crush their sales goals, allowing them to bring on more employees which often has required larger office spaces. Michelle's clients typically surpass their personal best in business development, often doubling their performance in the first year.

Michelle is the author of the Wall Street Journal Best Selling book, *The 29% Solution*, currently published in 7 languages and has contributed to two other books, *Make Your Connections Count* and *The World's Worst Networker*. She holds a Master's Degree in Adult Education, won an amateur bodybuilding contest in college and has completed two MS 150-mile bike rides.

Ever since she was a kid, Michelle as preferred to be outside any chance she gets. She favors being in her kayak on a lake with a fishing pole in her hand, remembering the countless hours she spent fishing with her dad and/or her grandpap by her side. She loves to walk her dogs, work in the garden, or make homemade wine. If you can't find her, she probably doesn't want to be found.

Patty Kreamer is a Certified Professional Organizer®, Productivity Coach and speaker who helps her clients reconnect with what is most important to them. Clients go from saying things like "I feel like I've missed my kid's childhood" to "I've attended every school play and soccer game for my son and daughter this year."

Patty is the author of ***But I Might Need It Someday*** and ***The Power of Simplicity*** as well as a co-author of ***Success Simplified*** with the late Stephen Covey. Patty was named Women's Business Network's Woman of the Year, one of Pennsylvania's Best 50 Women in Business and a Pittsburgh Fastracker.

Patty is a nationally sought-after speaker who is passionate, dynamic, and engaging. She is best known for her high energy, sense of humor, real-life success stories, and practical, useful information. She has personally improved the productivity and organization of thousands of lives through her written words, coaching, and speaking.

As a kid, Patty would alphabetize her Halloween candy from Almond Joy to Zagnut in shoe boxes. This carried her on to successfully running a professional organizing firm for 15 years. Before that, she was a teaching golf professional in the LPGA.

If you would like to inquire about having Michelle and Patty speak at your upcoming event, their coaching process for financial advisors, or if have any questions at all, please visit www.ProductivityUncorked.com or contact Michelle and Patty directly.

Michelle R. Donovan
Referral & Business Coach for Financial Advisors
Michelle@ProductivityUncorked.com
724-816-1760

Patty Kreamer
Productivity Coach for Financial Advisors
Patty@ProductivityUncorked.com
412-352-2888